A BRIEF HISTORY
OF THE UNIVERSITY OF CALIFORNIA

A BRIEF HISTORY
OF THE UNIVERSITY
OF CALIFORNIA

« « «   » » »

Second Edition

Revised and Expanded by

PATRICIA A. PELFREY
Center for Studies in Higher Education

UNIVERSITY OF CALIFORNIA
Berkeley, California

It is not the University of Berlin nor of New Haven which we are to copy . . . but it is the University of this State. It must be adapted to this people, to their public and private schools, to their peculiar geographical position, to the requirements of their new society and their undeveloped resources.

PRESIDENT DANIEL COIT GILMAN, 1872

CONTENTS

The original edition of *A Brief History of the University of California* was prepared as one of a series of publications marking the University's centennial in 1968. It was written by Margaret Cheney, although her name did not appear on the book. This second edition builds on Ms. Cheney's fine work by expanding some sections of the earlier *Brief History* and bringing the narrative up to 2004.

Both editions would have been impossible without the writings, personal recollections, assistance, and counsel of members of the University staff and faculty. Special thanks go to John Douglass, Sheldon Rothblatt, and others at the Center for Studies in Higher Education and in the Office of the President who gave me the benefit of their ideas, perspectives, and advice.

PATRICIA A. PELFREY

Berkeley 2004

*The College of California in Oakland gave impetus to the creation
of the University of California by offering to transfer all of
its lands, buildings, and books to the state in 1867.
Artist and source of drawing unknown.*

The University of California: What Makes It Unique?

Although the ministers, legislators, and entrepreneurs who labored to create the University looked eastward as far as Yale and even Oxford for their models, California's isolated geography and pioneering culture meant that the University of California would be different. The state had no long-standing tradition of private colleges and universities; it became an active and enthusiastic builder of public educational institutions early on.

The financial struggles of the young university notwithstanding, California went on to develop one of the nation's first organized and integrated systems of public higher education, its first network of community colleges, and its first multicampus research university—the University of California. Amid budget crises, political upheavals, and regional turf wars, a steady force propelling higher education forward was the California conviction, articulated most clearly by the Progressives early in the twentieth century, that education is a potent force in reshaping society and promoting prosperity. More than any other Americans, Californians believed in public education and were willing to pay for it. California's wealth, flowing first from its gold-laden mountains and rich agricultural valleys and later from the entrepreneurial talent of its citizens, gave the state the resources to pursue its dream of universal education.

Indispensable as they are, conviction and dollars alone would not have built a great university. The University of California's rise to eminence was the result of other fortunate circumstances besides the zeal of Californians for their land-grant institution. Among them must be counted UC's constitutional autonomy, which makes UC the legal equivalent of a fourth branch of state government. Though autonomy has never meant freedom from outside influence, at critical times it has been a strong shield against political winds.

The universitywide Academic Senate—the body that represents the faculty in the governance of UC—has long been among the most powerful in American higher education. Its insistence on rigorous peer review of faculty achievements, and its central role in governing the University, have ensured the primacy of academic quality and academic values. The presence of a universitywide senate, in addition to the senates on each campus, engenders a sense of unity in a huge and decentralized academic enterprise.

The organization of California higher education into a tripartite system under the 1960 Master Plan has freed each of the public segments—the California Community Colleges, the California State University (CSU), and UC—to concentrate on cultivating its own particular set of students as well as pursuing excellence in its assigned mission.

And UC's character as a multicampus system has been of overriding importance in its evolution. The University began as a single campus but became ten, a process that at times beat against the tide of opinion within and outside the UC community. The forced marriage of UC Berkeley and UC Los Angeles (UCLA) in the 1920s was the first step toward a confederation of research universities that differ from each other in many ways, yet are the same in several crucial respects. Every campus shares the same mandate for teaching, research, and public service and the same responsibility for demanding high academic standards. Unity of mission distinguishes UC from most other American multicampus systems. It has promoted competition *and* cooperation among the campuses, and that has in turn encouraged ambitious aspirations and high performance.

Every UC President since Robert Gordon Sproul has been forced to deal with the tension between the Office of the President and the campuses, and in the process to develop a perspective on the right balance between centralization and decentralization, oversight and independence. This dynamic tension has, in turn, required the University's leaders to rethink periodically what the University is and what it could be.

UC began as a small regional institution with big ideas about its future. Today it belongs not only to the society that created it but to the world, as one of just a handful of truly great universities. The University will always bear an indissoluble relationship to the State of California, however, because it is both a symbol and an engine of opportunity, that aspiration at the heart of the California dream.

No one has expressed this more eloquently than author and UC alumna Joan Didion. The University, she said, "seems to me more and more to be California's highest, most articulate idea of itself, the most coherent—perhaps the only coherent—expression of the California possibility."

Mind before Mines

The hope for a University of California was expressed at the first Constitutional Convention at Monterey in 1849—a year after the discovery of gold at Sutter's Mill and a year before California's admission to the Union.

In that year, the population of the territory almost doubled. The time was far from promising for a university movement, and action would await the arrival a few years later of a handful of churchmen sent by the American Home Missionary Society of New York to minister to human souls in the mining camps and boomtowns. Some of these men—for the most part Congregationalists and Presbyterians, their roots at Yale, Dartmouth, and the Union Theological Seminary of New York—remained to lay the cornerstones of higher education in California.

The new state, for all its natural wealth, lacked the means to support government and education. At the Constitutional Convention of 1849, the dilemma was stated:

> We are without a dollar belonging to the people, nor can we raise one but by levying taxes, which no population was ever in a worse condition to bear. In the lower portion of the territory . . . the laborers have abandoned their ranches and gone to the mines. Hence the owners of property . . . are nearly ruined by having to abandon their farms for want of laborers . . . the vast majority of people have no property to be taxed except the gold they dig out of the earth.

(And the gold, it was recognized, was almost impossible for the tax collector to lay hands on.)

Despite the odds against starting a university, some of the delegates to the first Convention were optimistic: "If we have the means here we can procure the necessary talent; we can bring the president of the Oxford University here by offering a sufficient salary."

The Convention petitioned Congress for public lands (later received) to be set apart for the use and support of a university; but it was to be almost two decades before such an institution was created.

To fill the vacuum, private schools and academies sprang up. The Contra Costa Academy opened in Oakland in 1853, and two years later it was incorporated as the College of California. The latter institution, through a transfer of its buildings and lands to the state, gave impetus to the creation of the University of California.

The University would be forever indebted to the churchmen and other citizens who guided the Academy and the College through the bogs of public apathy and around quicksands of perennial bankruptcy, never attempting sectarian control nor losing sight of the long-term goal—a university to serve the people of California.

"Mind before mines," exhorted the Rev. Dr. H. W. Bellows, a minister from the East who, as soon as he had surveyed the dismal prospect, wrote back to Yale and Harvard for suggestions. In the end, however, the interests of mind and mines were to be reconciled, to their mutual benefit.

Supporters in those early years included the Rev. S. H. Willey, who had arrived in 1849 for work in the territorial capital of Monterey; Sherman Day, the son of Yale's President Jeremiah Day; the Rev. Henry Durant of Yale—who was to become head of the College of California and first President of the University; and the Rev. Horace Bushnell, who came to California for his health but remained to search out potential sites for the future university.

Often despairing, they carried their dream to the new mansions of the frontier barons and periodically traveled to the East Coast on fund-raising drives.

"Durant out begging," was a common report.

Sometimes Durant lost patience:

Individuality is carried to an extreme in California. Our fast living may almost all of it be referred to intense selfishness. Indeed, sentimentality and idealism seem lost from the mass of the people. They are sensualists and materialists, or nearer that than anything else—the very condition on account of which the Spirit of God forsook the antediluvian world.

Land and a Charter

Debt stalked the College of California from the beginning, and bill collectors routinely waylaid Durant in the streets of Oakland.

Once when the college bell was to be repossessed by a San Francisco hardware dealer for the $100 still owed, three students asked for a leave of absence and managed to raise the sum. Despite the intense commitment of Durant, the students, trustees, and friends of the College, the future remained doubtful.

In 1853 Congress bestowed upon the state 46,000 acres of public lands, proceeds of the sale of which were to be used for a "seminary of learning." In 1862 the Morrill Act offered a grant of public lands to each state that would establish a college to teach agriculture and the mechanic arts—and California's share was 150,000 acres. Taking advantage of this grant, the state legislature in 1866 established an "Agricultural, Mining and Mechanic Arts College."

The new College had funds but no campus. The College of California had an adequate site, but limited funds. Therefore, when the College of California in 1867 offered its buildings and lands to the state on condition that a "complete university" be established to teach the humanities as well as agriculture, mining, and mechanics, the legislature accepted. The act of 1866 was repealed and a new act passed. Signed by Governor H. H. Haight on March 23, 1868—Charter Day— the new act created the University of California.

The College property, in addition to the Oakland site, included land for a new campus among the oak trees and open fields, four miles to the north.

After prolonged deliberation by leaders of the university movement, the surrounding townsite was named for George Berkeley, Bishop of Cloyne, who had visited America in 1729 in the hope of founding an educational institution for the evangelization and education of "aboriginal Americans." Finding the time not right, he had provided the model for Columbia University and endowed three scholarships at Yale.

He is the author of the poem whose last three stanzas hold a special meaning for Californians:

> There shall be sung another golden Age,
> The rise of Empire and of Arts,
> The Good and Great inspiring epic Rage,
> The wisest Heads and noblest Hearts.
>
> Not such as *Europe* breeds in her decay;
> Such as she bred when fresh and young,
> When heav'nly Flame did animate her Clay,
> By future Poets shall be sung.
>
> Westward the Course of Empire takes its Way;
> The four first Acts already past.
> A fifth shall close the Drama with the Day;
> Time's noblest Offspring is the last.

The Twelve Apostles, graduates of the Class of 1873, would become distinguished citizens and public servants. Left to right, standing, are J. B. Reinstein, later a Regent; Frank Otis, Mayor of Alameda; James H. Budd, Congressional Representative and Governor of California; Thomas P. Woodward, engineer and educator; Clarence Wetmore, businessman; and Nathan Neumark, attorney. Seated are George C. Edwards, professor of mathematics; L. L. Hawkins, bank president; Franklin Rhoda, clergyman; Ebenezer Scott, businessman; George J. Ainsworth, Regent; and John M. Bolton, rancher.
Photograph courtesy University Archives.

The University

The 1868 act establishing the University entrusted its organization and government to a corporate body titled the Regents of the University of California.

The Board of Regents is composed of twenty-six members, eighteen appointed by the Governor for twelve-year terms, one student appointed by the Regents to a one-year term, and seven who are members because of offices they hold. These ex officio members are the Governor, the Lieutenant Governor, the Speaker of the Assembly, the State Superintendent of Public Instruction, the President and Vice President of the Alumni Associations of the University of California, and the President of the University. In addition, two faculty representatives participate in the Board's discussions but do not vote. More than four hundred Californians have served as Regents since the University's founding in 1868.

The "tiny band of scholars" on hand when the University opened in Oakland in 1869 included ten faculty members and thirty-eight students. Several of the students had been enrolled in the College of California. Graduates of the College legally became alumni of the University in 1868. Of the University's charter class, twelve were graduated in 1873, to be known thereafter as the "Twelve Apostles." Classes began at Berkeley in 1873 on completion of North and South Halls (the latter building still stands).

The Regents of the University touched off a furor when they invited as first president Civil War General George B. McClellan, who had opposed Abraham Lincoln for the presidency of the United States in 1864. Among newspapers, one of the few to support the election of General McClellan was the San Francisco *Examiner,* which protested, "We want no narrow-brained, fanatical sectionalist of New England optimism and puritanism to preside over our cosmopolitan University."

General McClellan declined the honor, however, and in 1870, the Regents unanimously elected Professor Daniel Coit Gilman of the Sheffield Scientific School at Yale. He was told, "We pay $6,000 in gold, to which in due season a house will be added." But Gilman was then deeply involved in his work at Yale and also declined. Thereupon, Henry Durant was elected first President, taking over from John LeConte, who had been serving in an acting capacity.

John and Joseph LeConte, who had served during the Civil War as chemists in factories of the Confederacy, came to the University as scholars of international renown with high recommendations from eastern universities. They were to contribute brilliantly to the development of the institution during its first three decades. John, who had been a professor of physics at the University of South Carolina, taught industrial mechanics. Joseph, from the same institution, served as professor of geology, botany, and natural history. The University's offerings were sparse in the beginning. "Announced lectures on political economy, history of civilization, and international law, were expressions of a hope rather than of a realized state of things," noted William Carey Jones, an early chronicler of the University.[1]

The Regents passed a resolution in 1870 declaring that women would be admitted to the University equally with men. Eight women registered for UC in the fall. Four years later, President Gilman was to remark that the proportion of women who ranked high in scholarship was greater than that of men. Jones, writing about coeducation in 1895, remarked, "If any have doubts about its expediency, they cannot draw any arguments against it from our experience in California."[2]

President Gilman

In 1872 President Durant resigned, stating he believed a younger man could better advance the interests of the University. Once again, the Regents turned to Daniel Coit Gilman of Yale, who, this time, and to the lasting good fortune of the University, accepted the appointment.

A distinguished educator sought by many universities, Gilman served the University of California for three turbulent years. He was excited by the prospect of building a university in a young state untrammeled by tradition. Unfortunately, his term was beset by financial difficulties and political harassment that culminated in a legislative investigation. Yet he perceived the true nature of a great university and laid down guidelines for its development.

Two things, he asserted, were settled by the Charter of the University of California and embodied in the name it bore.

"First it is a university, and not a high school nor a college, nor an academy of sciences nor an industrial school which we are charged to build," he declared in the University's first inaugural address.

> Some of these features may indeed be included . . .
> but the university means more than any or all of them.
> The university is the most comprehensive term which
> can be employed to indicate a foundation for the pro-
> motion and diffusion of knowledge. . . . It is not the
> University of Berlin nor of New Haven which we are
> to copy . . . but it is the University of this State. It
> must be adapted to this people, to their public and
> private schools, to their peculiar geographical position,
> to the requirements of their new society and their
> undeveloped resources.

President Gilman saw the University's graduates as the nucleus of the future not only of California but of a vast region—"the new civilization of the Pacific coast"—and was concerned that they be equipped with the most comprehensive culture that could be provided.

"Science is the mother of California," he said.

> Give us more and not less science; encourage the
> most thorough and prolonged search for the truth
> which is to be found in the rocks, the sea, the soil,
> the air, the sun and the stars; in light and heat and
> magnetic forces; in plants and animals and in the
> human frame; but let us also learn the lessons which
> are embodied in language and literature, in laws and
> institutions, in doctrines and opinions, in historical
> progress.

Gilman soon found himself confronted with a crisis: the University's very existence was jeopardized by long-simmering conflicts over whose interests it was to serve. Criticism centered on the relative emphases to be laid, or being laid, on the literary, agricultural, and scientific departments. Advocates for agricultural interests contended that the University was failing in its obligations under the Morrill Land-Grant College Act to provide education in the "agricultural and mechanic arts." Defenders, President Gilman among them, argued that the University was hospitable to the needs of California's farmers, but that its approach to agricultural education must be based on scientific study and methods of inquiry, not on vocational training for future farmers.

A legislative investigation of alleged mismanagement of the University's land-grant funds was undertaken. Although

Women students were admitted to the University in 1870. Photograph courtesy University Archives.

it resulted in the return of a clean ledger, it affirmed that there had been a want of clear understanding both as to the grant and the management of the University.

The University had scraped by, but Gilman found the heat of the battle too blistering for his taste. The University, he said, "is . . . nominally administered by the Regents; it is virtually administered by the legislature." Frustrated, he offered his resignation in 1874 but was dissuaded by the Regents. The following year, however, the offer of the presidency of Johns Hopkins University was too great a temptation, and he accepted it.

Gilman did more than fight the University's battles in the public arena during his brief but momentous tenure. He laid the foundations for the future by instituting the University's first visiting lectureships and graduate fellowships, doubling the size of its library, and defining the standards to which it should aspire. Looking back on his California experience in later years, Gilman said that he had "helped rescue a state university from the limitations of a college of agriculture and enlarge it to meet the requirements of a magnificent commonwealth."[3]

The Constitutional Convention
of 1878

The University's troubles with its constituencies persisted throughout the 1870s. It was a time of intense political agitation in California, fanned by economic instability, charges of legislative corruption, and headlong population growth. Many believed a new constitution, revised to better reflect the society California had become after thirty years of statehood, would be a constructive step to address the state's ills. In September 1878, delegates met in Sacramento for California's Second Constitutional Convention.

As the convention settled down to work, the University's position was precarious. Some of the earlier charges of mismanagement were revived, and the University was once again attacked by agrarian and labor groups as a bastion of elitism. One proposal was to give the legislature direct authority over the University; another was to elect a majority of the Regents by popular vote. A third was to disband the University entirely and start afresh with an institution devoted exclusively to practical rather than classical education.

But the University had two distinct advantages. The Convention's education committee included two Regents, one of whom—Joseph Winans—was the chair. Winans argued persuasively that a university vulnerable to "sectarian and political designs . . . will never flourish." Just as important, however, was the deep-seated unhappiness with the legislature that prevailed among the delegates. They ultimately decided to entrust the University's fate to its own hands.

By a narrow vote, the University was made a public trust and its autonomy guaranteed under the new State Constitution, approved by the voters on May 17, 1879. Article IX, section 9, gives the Regents "full powers of organization and government, subject only to such Legislative control as may be necessary to insure compliance with the terms of the endowments of the University and the security of its funds." The University is to be "entirely independent of all political or sectarian influence, and kept free therefrom in the appointment of its regents and in the administration of its affairs." The provision bestows upon the University of California a degree of independence shared by few other public institutions in the nation—a fact that had a decisive effect on its future.

By the end of the turbulent 1870s, the University had successfully weathered major threats to its organization and mission, and essentially charted its course. UC would meet its obligations to serve the needs of agriculture and other sectors of the state's growing economy, but it would do so in ways appropriate to a research university and consistent with providing a broad liberal education to its students.

Early Benefactors

The University's financial problems seemed endless. Early on, it was hoped that income from the permanent endowment of the University would meet most of its operating costs. In 1887, however, the legislature found it necessary to levy a cent of tax on every $100 of taxable property in the state to augment this income. A decade later, the tax advanced to two cents; yet, in the early years, it was seldom easy to get the necessary appropriations for the University.

Many years were to pass, too, before the citizens of California gave large donations to their University; but even the smallest of those first gifts was important. In 1871, for example, a gift of $500 bought a modern encyclopedia and numerous volumes of history and literature.

As Californians began to feel a personal pride in the University, they created a tradition of generous private support. Indeed, most of the early buildings on the Berkeley campus were the result of gifts. Until 1940, more than half of all the lands and buildings of the University were purchased as a result of donations from private sources.

The first large benefaction came from Edward Tompkins of Oakland, one of the first Regents. Aware of the new commerce opening up between California and Asia, he gave property—to be held until it became worth $50,000—for the Agassiz Professorship of Oriental Languages.

At a time when immigrants of any nationality were apt to be received coldly in California—if not excluded outright—Mr. Tompkins expressed the desire that the University make education available for such young men as might come to this country from Asia.

"I feel deeply the humiliation," he said, "of seeing them pass by us in almost daily procession to the other side of the continent in search of that intellectual hospitality which we are not yet enlightened enough to extend to them."

Foreign students began to enroll at the University in the 1870s. Six decades later the University received a gift of

$1,750,000 from John D. Rockefeller Jr. to establish an International House at Berkeley. Today, UC's systemwide foreign student enrollment of 8,000 from nearly 150 countries is the largest in the nation.

The University's first great scientific station—the Lick Observatory on Mount Hamilton—was a nineteenth-century gift from the colorful San Franciscan James Lick. The observatory, which is the site of a 120-inch telescope, is well known for its research into the evolution of stars, the history of the galaxy, and other mysteries of space that have intrigued mankind. In 1965 the Santa Cruz campus took over operation of Lick.

A gift of immense importance was that of Dr. H. H. Toland, who in 1873 donated the Toland Medical College in San Francisco, consisting of property worth about $100,000, to the University for use as a medical school.

An immigrant Bavarian leather tanner named Michael Reese, who had acquired a fortune in San Francisco real estate, left $50,000 to the library in 1878. Hastings College of Law in San Francisco was established by the legislature with generous financial assistance from Judge Serranus Clinton Hastings, the first Chief Justice of California, who paid $100,000 into the state treasury on condition that the state pay annual interest of seven percent toward maintaining the school.

Henry Douglas Bacon of Oakland presented the University with his art collection, together with funds to aid in construction of the Bacon Art and Library Building. Another Oakland resident, A. K. P. Harmon, gave the University the original Harmon Gymnasium. Today the sports facility, renovated and expanded to nearly twice its original size, is known as the Walter A. Haas Jr. Pavilion.

Formation of student battalion in front of Bacon
Art and Library Building in the 1890s.
Photograph courtesy University Archives.

Phoebe Apperson Hearst, who became a Regent in 1897, was a benefactress of great generosity. In 1891 she endowed five scholarships for "worthy young women." Later, she provided funds for the University's first comprehensive building plan and for two buildings at Berkeley, including the Hearst Memorial Mining Building, which is dedicated to the memory of her husband, Senator George Hearst.

The comprehensive building plan invited international competition. In 1898, 105 designs were submitted for the preliminary round, held at the Royal Museum in Antwerp. During the second round, held in California two years later, architect Emile Bénard was selected as the winner. His grandiose plan for a series of Beaux Arts buildings with a central avenue oriented toward the Golden Gate was never fully carried out; problems with Bénard and his plan surfaced early on, and he was soon replaced by one of the other finalists in the competition, American architect John Galen Howard.

Howard put his own distinctive stamp on Bénard's vision and adapted his plan to the contours of the Berkeley site. Under Howard's guidance, new buildings soon transformed the landscape, among them the Charles Franklin Doe Memorial Library, Wheeler Hall, and Hilgard Hall. A gift of $100,000 from Mrs. John H. Boalt, in memory of her husband, made possible the construction of a law building, Boalt Hall. In 1951 the name was transferred to a larger building to accommodate the growing law school, and the original Boalt Hall was renamed Durant Hall.

Jane K. Sather, in memory of her husband, Peder—who had been a trustee of the College of California—endowed two professorships and gave to the campus two of its enduring landmarks, Sather Tower, generally known as the Campanile, and Sather Gate.

These were but a few of the generous benefactions so important to the University in the early decades.

Growth for the Twentieth Century

The approach of a new century brought a quicker tempo and a broadening responsiveness by the University to the needs of the state and the nation. In the first few decades of the University's existence, enrollment grew extraordinarily, as did the resources for effective teaching. Although the first two years of undergraduate study continued to be general in nature, the variety of upper-division courses rapidly increased.

Isolated by geography from the great eastern centers of learning, the University was developing the distinctive California characteristics of restlessness and seam-bursting vigor.

Agriculture, the humanities, and most of all, engineering, were to form the bases of its early claims to fame.

Scholars and scientists of international reputation were attracted to Berkeley. Eugene W. Hilgard, one of the nation's great geologists and soil chemists, joined the faculty in 1875 and laid the foundations of the College of Agriculture. He was a vigorous advocate of scientific agriculture who won over skeptical farmers to the University's cause through his ceaseless activity on behalf of California agriculture.

Five years earlier, the Regents had recognized the need for agricultural extension by authorizing "the Professor of Agriculture" to visit as many agricultural centers in the state as possible and extend to them the advantages of the College.

Samuel B. Christy became Dean of the College of Mining in 1885 and took on the responsibility of laying out laboratories for one of the first adequately equipped mining schools in the world. Under his direction, the reputation of the College was firmly established; soon students were coming from lands as distant as Peru and South Africa. Frank H. Probert, an English mining engineer who became Dean in 1917, continued the tradition of strong leadership.

The College of Civil Engineering also performed notable service in building the young state. Shortly after the turn of the century, Engineering added a Department of Irrigation headed by the international authority Elwood Mead, whose advice was constantly in demand by countries plagued with the problems of a dry climate. Later on, under Charles Derleth, the College would be called upon by the federal government in the planning stages of such mammoth projects as the Hoover Dam and the Golden Gate and Bay Bridges.

Science, in the early years, was mainly centered in the College of Chemistry, where the foundations were well laid by a few eminent scientists. In 1912 Gilbert N. Lewis joined the staff to serve with distinction as professor of physical chemistry and Dean of the College.

By the middle 1890s, Charles Mills Gayley was building an English department that would become famous. Henry Morse Stephens, before his death in 1919—and after him, Herbert E. Bolton—made the study of history and California seem almost synonymous. Alexis Lange, who became Dean of the School of Education, was the father of the 1907 legislation establishing California's system of junior—now community—colleges.

In 1893, the University of California Press was founded for the dual purpose of stimulating research and publishing it. Today UC Press is the largest publishing arm of any public university in the country and one of the most distinguished anywhere.

San Franciscans were eager to develop trade with Asia, and Berkeley's College of Commerce was originally intended to train students for the export trade. Almost immediately, however, it enjoyed a more broadly based success. Industry and business throughout the state also wanted college-trained individuals. The opening of the Panama Canal in 1915 stimulated California's commerce with Europe and South America, resulting in still greater enrollments in the College.

Secretary of State Elihu Root, in the first decade of the new century, called attention to the poor quality of America's consular officers, then largely political appointees, and the University responded with a course for the training of foreign service personnel.

Among new departments created early in the century were anatomy, anthropology, architecture, biochemistry, household art, household science, hygiene, physiology, Sanskrit, and

Slavic languages. There was a vigorous expansion of existing departments. The Department of History and Political Science became three: history, political science, and economics.

The University summer sessions, begun in 1899 to train teachers in physics and chemistry, met with an enthusiastic response.

Although scientific research was accelerating, the University's leading scholars—like their counterparts at most American universities—remained more oriented toward teaching than research. With the exception of government-sponsored research in agriculture, scientific activity would remain comparatively small in scale and in financial support until the surge of the 1930s.

Yet as early as 1910, it was clear that something remarkable was under way at the University of California. In that year, Edwin E. Slosson published a book titled *Great American Universities,* which focused on ten outstanding American institutions of higher education. The University of California was among them. Professor Slosson's assessment of the University reflected how productively it had resolved the conflict over practical versus classical education:

> I know of no other university which cultivates both
> mechanics and metaphysics with such equal success,
> or which looks so far into space, and, at the same time,
> comes so close to the lives of the people; or which exca-
> vates the tombs of the Pharaohs and Incas while it is
> inventing new plants for the agriculture of the future.[4]

Further, Slosson was struck by the diversity of foreign students at Berkeley relative to that of other universities he visited. "There is a new form of university coming," he wrote, "which is foreshadowed in California. Greater and more influential than a State or a national university will be the international university of the future."[5]

President Wheeler

Author Irving Stone tells of arriving on the Berkeley campus in 1920, pausing to look up at Wheeler Hall, and being depressed suddenly by the sense that he did not belong there, that he had not enough money to get through the first year, and that he would probably fail in science and mathematics.

"Then as I was about to turn away, feeling lonely, dejected, and unwanted," he relates,

an apparition appeared on the hill above me: a man on horseback, wearing a black hat, a loose black cape. I thought for a moment that the shock of entering the campus had created some kind of hallucination.

As the figure rode slowly toward me, I perceived that it was one of the most beautiful human beings I had ever seen. There was a warm, gentle smile on his face; his cheeks were red, and his expression alive and excited; he was obviously of considerable age.

The figure on horseback swept off his hat, bowed from the saddle, said, "Good evening, sir," and moved on down the road.

I stood there, literally transfixed. No one before had ever called me "sir." It was not only that I had, by the one word, been transformed from a child into an adult, but also that I had been promoted somehow from the lower middle class into a top echelon of gentlemen and scholars.

Stone remained and graduated with the Class of 1923.

The figure was President Emeritus Benjamin Ide Wheeler. He had come to the University in 1899—an eminent scholar, a man of immense vigor—and served as its head for twenty years. They were booming years for the University, and President Wheeler was ideally suited to the times.

When he arrived he found the University woefully under-funded for the tasks he believed it should pursue. Educated at the University of Heidelberg, he was an admirer of research-oriented German education and believed deeply that the University of California would remain an incomplete institution until it incorporated a comprehensive and vigorous research enterprise. He insisted upon having authority for hiring and setting faculty salaries, and the Regents agreed.[6]

Under his leadership the University made great strides in both research and public service. Graduate work expanded and was formally recognized in the establishment of the Graduate Division. And he recruited top-notch faculty from around the country to improve the University's academic standing and standards.

Wheeler worked hard and successfully to bolster state support for the University. During the Wheeler years, the University acquired its first million-dollar budget. His persuasive fund-raising skills attracted further support, especially for building, from the wealthy and the well born. He recognized the necessity of a great library and systematically built the University's collections.

Students flocked to the University in record numbers during the Wheeler era. When he became President, there were 2,600 students; by the time of his retirement in 1919, that figure had mushroomed to more than 12,000. Self-government by the student body had begun in 1887 when the Associated Students of the College of Letters and Science

California Hall and the Campanile, soon after its construction in 1917. Photograph courtesy University Archives.

was organized. Early generations of students were a lively lot, and it was President Wheeler who initiated a system that finally proved satisfactory to all. Under "senior rule," the senior class became the real disciplinary and law-making body. So effective did this system prove that the faculty in practice gave up all but an advisory role.

During that period the University began the lateral growth that has accelerated through the years. The University Farm was established at Davis, the Citrus Experiment Station at Riverside, the Scripps Institution for Biological Research (later the Scripps Institution of Oceanography) at La Jolla, and the Hooper Foundation for Medical Research at San Francisco. The "Southern Branch" of the University at Los Angeles was just beginning to emerge. University Extension, established in 1892, matured rapidly during President Wheeler's administration.

Wheeler had a special feeling for students. "The only thing that is of interest to me in a university," he said, "is men and women." He regarded the University community as a family bound together by love for its alma mater and the primary purpose of education as the formation of character.

In the final years of his tenure, however, Wheeler's health was uncertain and his conflicts with the faculty grew—it is said that a faculty member who did not wear a hat on campus risked a reprimand from the President. His pro-German views in the era of the First World War did nothing to add to his popularity. In 1919, he was forced to resign.[7]

Today Wheeler is remembered as a great university builder. He is also honored for what he himself regarded as a university's noblest work—educating responsible and enlightened citizens.

The Faculty Revolution

The number of UC faculty members tripled from 202 to 693 during the Wheeler era. By the end of his productive but authoritarian presidency, the faculty had become restive over its relative powerlessness in the affairs of the University. The Regents' decision to create a three-person administrative board to run the University pending the appointment of a new President brought matters to a head. On October 3, 1919, the Academic Senate sent a polite memorandum to the Regents laying out its proposals for change. In essence, the faculty asked for more control over matters within its purview and for a greater voice in decisions made by the President and the Regents.

Negotiations between the faculty and the Regents continued into the following spring. On June 24, 1920, the Regents adopted new Standing Orders that formally recognized the Academic Senate and its role in the governance of the Uni-

Upper left: Henry Durant, President, 1870–72. Upper right: Daniel Coit Gilman, President, 1872–75. Lower left: John LeConte, President, 1876–81. Lower right: Benjamin Ide Wheeler, President, 1899–1919. Photographs courtesy University Archives.

versity. Most important was the provision that the Senate (rather than the President) "shall choose its own . . . committees"—an authorization that has been called the "cornerstone of the Senate's power" because it established the Senate's independence.[8] The faculty revolt of 1919–20 was a historic step toward the system of shared governance among faculty, administration, and Regents that has played such a prominent part in the development of the University.

Growth of the Campuses

In 1923 the University of California, with 14,061 full-time students, led the universities of the United States and the world in enrollment. By the end of the 1920s it had conferred more than 40,000 degrees. Its alumni included four Governors of California and several United States senators and congressmen. Other graduates were occupying positions of responsibility in all avenues of life and in many parts of the world.

Westward migration was swelling the population of California and the University was hard-pressed to grow quickly enough. Primarily because of rapid development of the Southern Branch, Professor David Prescott Barrows of the Department of Political Science, who succeeded President Wheeler, signaled his induction into office by presenting the University with its first red-ink budget—red ink to the extent of half a million dollars.

The reaction from the Regents was, "It doesn't seem to be enough." Thereupon, President Barrows increased the deficit to $670,000 and received the Board's approval. An initiative measure that would have provided an income from the state of more than four million dollars was submitted to the voters in 1920. Although failing to pass by a narrow margin, it paved the way for financial subsidy by legislative act a few months later.

The geographic size and shape of the state and the growth pattern of its cities created a need not only for a large campus at Los Angeles, but also for smaller ones to serve other regions. For these new campuses, there would not be the protracted growing pains that had accompanied the development of Berkeley. The need was better established in the public mind. Legislatures were generous in their support; alumni and other citizens gave liberally of the extras that made the difference between the merely adequate and the exceptional.

The Modern University

William Wallace Campbell, a professor of astronomy and for many years director of Lick Observatory, served as President of the University in the important years 1923-30. His administration was characterized by steady growth and rising enrollments, the latter trend continuing even when the onset of the Depression foreshadowed a curtailment of physical development.

Until the 1930s, the University remained a lively but predominantly regional institution. If one year can be said to have marked a turning point, it was 1934. That year the American Council on Education asked 2,000 leading scholars of the United States to analyze the graduate schools of the nation's universities.

The survey covered thirty-six fields of learning. Universities were rated on the basis of their "distinguished" or "adequate" departments. For the first time, the Ivy League was compelled to acknowledge serious competition in the West. The University of California rated as many distinguished and

*Wheeler Oak and
Steps, a favorite
gathering place
in the 1920s.
Photograph courtesy
University Archives.*

adequate departments as any university in the country. This
was only the beginning of a great surge forward.

President Sproul

Robert Gordon Sproul, described by *Time* magazine as "a Californian both by birth and inclination," became the first
native son and alumnus of the University to serve as its President. He was to guide its fortunes longer than any of his
predecessors (or successors to date)—through three cata-
clysmic decades that included the Depression, World War II,
and the birth of the atomic bomb. And he was to see the University attain world renown for scientific achievement in a
period when the body of scientific knowledge began to expand
at a rate unprecedented in history.

A graduate of the Berkeley campus with a degree in civil engineering, Sproul was hired to fill a position in the Berkeley cashier's office vacated by a clerk who had run off with some University funds. Sproul became Vice President and Controller at the age of thirty-four. In addition, he served as Secretary of the Regents. As an undergraduate at the University, he had been active in student affairs and athletics; as President, he demonstrated an intuitive grasp of the problems of the undergraduate.

Few could match his phenomenal energy or his charisma as a speaker. None exceeded him in skill at winning over legislative critics and converting them into staunch allies of the University.

When President Sproul assumed office in 1930, UC had become the first major university in the country to transform itself into a multicampus institution. The problem of maintaining unity of purpose and spirit among the diverse segments had assumed major proportions. For many years, President Sproul spent about half of his time at Berkeley, a third at Los Angeles, and the rest among the other campuses. In 1936, he and his family transferred their main residence to Los Angeles for a year. At the annual football contest between Berkeley and UCLA, President Sproul would sit on the Cal side until half-time, and then stride across the field, escorted by the student band, to the Bruin side for the remainder of the game.

From the beginning, President Sproul hammered away at a single theme. The University of California must be able to compete for the top faculty members—not merely with other universities in California but with the leading institutions in the country. His powers of persuasion in the legislature were such that UC was able to match, in salaries and in the facilities for teaching and research, the best that eastern universities could offer. Over the years, he attracted a brilliant array of talent in virtually every branch of learning.

A spectacular example is Sproul's decision to persuade Ernest O. Lawrence to resist the blandishments of a rival university that had promised him funds for the expensive equipment he needed to further his pathbreaking research in high-energy physics. Sproul agreed to match the offer, and Lawrence stayed at Berkeley. In 1929 Lawrence invented the cyclotron, the first of a succession of atom smashers, in recognition of which he was awarded the Nobel Prize ten years later. The war in Europe kept him from attending the Nobel ceremonies, but he was honored with a celebration in Berkeley and a party in San Francisco that included a cake shaped like his cyclotron.

The brilliant and charismatic Lawrence was a transformational figure both in the University and in the larger world of science. His fame brought national renown to the University (his Nobel Prize was UC's first) as the admiring and the curious flocked to meet "the man who smashes atoms." At a time when most researchers pursued their scientific interests in isolation, he had the bold idea of organizing scientists into teams that crossed disciplinary boundaries, creating an enormous gain in investigative power. The success of Lawrence's interdisciplinary approach ultimately shaped the way science was conducted worldwide.

Today the Lawrence Berkeley National Laboratory is known not only for its work in high-energy physics but for advances in many scientific disciplines. No other laboratory of its scale is as closely integrated with a university; the intellectual stimulation faculty and students bring contributes to solving problems of national and international significance.

The University's contribution to national defense began in

*Robert Gordon Sproul,
President, 1930–58.
Photograph courtesy
University Archives.*

the late 1930s. With the advent of World War II, every campus became a center of research and training. Thousands of members of the academic community were granted leave to engage in war work, to join the armed forces, or to devote full time to scientific research. Under the University War Training Program, the campuses and University Extension undertook the technical training of manpower for California war industries. Vitally needed research went into the improvement of nutrition for the civilian and military population, into medicine and public health, and into the social and physical sciences. Out of this effort came major breakthroughs, notably in the health and physical sciences.

The University's most far-reaching contribution to the war effort was its involvement in the Manhattan Project. The UC-operated Los Alamos Scientific Laboratory produced the first atomic bombs, whose use hastened the end of the war in the Pacific but also came as a shocking revelation of humanity's power to destroy. Sproul's vigorous optimism remained unshaken. "After all," he said, "the greatest human power in the world today is not the atomic bomb. The human mind that conceived the bomb is a greater power by far, and the university which is the citadel of that mind is still a mighty fortress on which we may rely for the perpetuity of a society of free men."[9]

In 1949 the Soviet Union detonated an atomic bomb, a milestone event that led to the founding of a second nuclear weapons laboratory three years later in Livermore to broaden U.S. expertise and keep American science abreast of future discoveries. Both laboratories played critical roles in defense and nuclear deterrence during the ensuing decades. Both are now among the world's premier science centers. Since the end of the Cold War in the 1980s, they have expanded their focus to include nondefense research important to the nation, including work on environmental issues, exploration of the human genome, and laser fusion energy.

The Loyalty Oath

The postwar years, marked by McCarthyism and the Red scare, brought a painful crisis to President Sproul's administration and the University. In 1949, several controversial incidents on the Los Angeles campus roused the Regents' concern, among them speaking invitations to left-leaning British Labour Party member Harold Laski and to a professor who had been dismissed from the University of Washington because of his membership in the Communist Party. In the politically charged climate of the times, President Sproul urged the Regents to adopt a loyalty oath that would implement the University's 1940 policy prohibiting the employment of Communists, a recommendation the Board accepted in the spring of 1949. Although President Sproul soon regretted his action and faculty resistance to the oath spread, the Regents reaffirmed and upheld the oath in March 1950. Thirty-one faculty members were dismissed that same year for refusing to sign it.

When the courts ruled the oath invalid almost two years later, offers of reinstatement were made to these thirty-one faculty. In the meantime, however, the legislature voted to impose a loyalty oath of its own, known as the Levering Oath, that all state employees were required to sign as a condition of employment—and do to this day.

The loyalty oath episode was a manifestation of the politics of the times, but it also became a dispute over governance of the University, as the President found himself caught in the middle between Regents and faculty. To those members of the public who were convinced the Communist threat at UC was real, the University seemed vacillating and untrustworthy; to those worried about academic freedom, it appeared unwilling to defend its own deepest values.

Progress and Problems

Despite its lingering effects, the loyalty oath crisis did not check the dramatic rise in the University's academic standing during the postwar years. The faculty had long excelled in the number of recipients of Guggenheim Fellowships. By the end of the 1950s, UC led every other university and university system in the nation in the number of faculty members elected to the National Academy of Sciences.

The library at Berkeley was exceeded only by the Library of Congress and Harvard University for the quality of its collections. The UCLA library, one of the youngest in the country, was also one of the most rapidly growing, having passed the one-million mark in 1953.

Physical development of the campuses, which had lagged during the Depression and been further delayed by war, boomed during the 1940s and '50s. It had to, for the University anticipated an immediate swell in the form of huge veteran enrollments and a subsequent period of sustained growth.

Between 1944 and 1958, the University acquired the Santa Barbara campus and developed liberal arts colleges at Davis and Riverside. The medical school at Los Angeles was begun in that period. Meanwhile, graduate programs were expanding swiftly and there was great demand for postdoctoral training in the medical and physical sciences.

In California and throughout the nation a new tide was running in student demand for college admission. At the beginning of Sproul's long presidency, new state and community colleges had begun springing up everywhere. Each session of the California legislature brought greater pressure and competition for new campuses and budgets. President Sproul recognized that, unless means could be found for their orderly development, the institutions of public higher education faced a potentially disastrous course of competition.

He saw this as a national problem, but one that held particular urgency for rapidly growing California. In 1931, he had persuaded the Regents and the legislature to provide matching funds for a study by the Carnegie Foundation. The result was one of three studies undertaken during ensuing decades— the other two were the 1947 *Strayer Committee Report* and the

1953 *Restudy of the Needs of California in Higher Education*—
that led, finally, to the 1960 *Master Plan for Higher Education
in California.*

Robert Gordon Sproul retired in 1958. During his twenty-eight years in office, many tried to induce him to consider posts that ranged from the presidency of a bank to directorship of the Prune and Apricot Growers organization to political office in the U.S. Congress or even the White House. Although he recognized these offers as a tribute to his leadership, he once described them as a "nuisance." He was—first, last, and always—President of the University of California.

The Chancellorship

In the early days of the University, most administrative authority was centered in the Board of Regents. The 1868 Organic Act described the President as "the executive head of the institution in all its departments," but in fact the President's authority was largely limited to academic areas. In 1890, for example, it took a special amendment to the Regents' bylaws to give the President authority to hire, dismiss, and regulate the duties of janitors. Replacement of a lost diploma required attention from the Regents until 1901.[10] It was only during the administration of Benjamin Ide Wheeler (1899–1920) that the President truly became the chief executive officer of the University.

During President Sproul's long tenure, the issue of how the University was to reorganize itself to deal with its transformation into a multicampus system surfaced several times and with increasing urgency. The University and Berkeley were no longer the same thing. UCLA, the Southern Branch, was becoming a full-fledged campus. The University was growing

Clark Kerr, President, 1958–67.
Photograph courtesy Gabriel Moulin Studio,
San Francisco.

and its research and extension activities were multiplying up and down the state.

A 1948 report on governance pointed out that lines of responsibility and communication among the campus heads, the President, and the Regents were cloudy at best. Most administrative decision-making power, including authority over campus budgets and the hiring and firing of faculty members, rested with the President. The burdens on his office were enormous and growing. The report estimated that 200 to 500 items routinely languished in the President's office without a decision, and that the University's "administrative arrangements" were "fashioned for days gone by."[11] It concluded that the Board of Regents was too enmeshed in administrative detail as well, and recommended wide-ranging delegation of authority from the Board to the administration.

Sproul was reluctant to make major changes in the University's organization and governance, however. He was comfortable with his role, despite the staggering workload, and he feared that delegating significant authority to individual campuses would threaten institutional unity—the "One University" ideal to which he was deeply committed. When the provosts at the two major campuses, Berkeley and UCLA, were designated Chancellors in 1951, the scope of their authority did not match the grandeur of their new titles. In practice, UC remained an institution governed from the center. Yet the University had moved a critical step down the road to decentralization.

The Multiversity

Clark Kerr (1958–67) was the first UC President who had also been a Chancellor. He brought a new perspective to the leadership of the University, shaped not only by his experience as a chief campus officer but also by his years as a professor of economics and labor relations on the Berkeley campus, a labor mediator, and head of the campus's Institute of Industrial Relations. Kerr had a singular ability to look at mountains of information and discern patterns and trends where others saw only a jumble of unrelated facts and statistics. He was a particularly acute observer of higher education. In his Godkin Lectures, delivered at Harvard University in 1963, he presented a magisterial view of the American research university at midcentury. The traditional university of the past, he said, had been succeeded by a new kind of institution—the multiversity:

The University started as a single community—a community of masters and students. It may even be said to have had a soul in the sense of a central animating principle. Today the large American university is, rather, a whole series of communities and activities held together by a common name, a common governing board, and related purposes. This great transformation is regretted by some, accepted by many, gloried in, as yet, by few. But it should be understood by all.[12]

The fragmentation of the university into the many-purposed multiversity served the needs of postwar society, in which knowledge was growing exponentially and becoming a vital economic commodity. The research university, connected at multiplying points to government and industry, was thrust into new responsibilities that it was more than willing to accept.

The price for the university—its growing impersonality and loss of community—was balanced by the exuberant energy and sheer productivity of this new entity, which had "no living peers in the search for new knowledge; and no peers in all history in serving so many of the segments of an advancing civilization." Kerr described the progress of the American multiversity in a way that united admiration with unease:

The multiversity has demonstrated how adaptive it can be to new opportunities for creativity; how responsive to money; how eagerly it can play a new and useful role; how fast it can change while pretending that nothing has happened at all; how fast it can neglect some of its ancient virtues.[13]

One observation was to ring with special meaning a few years later: "The multiversity is a confusing place for the student.

He has problems of establishing his identity and sense of security within it. . . . The casualty rate is high. The walking wounded are many."[14]

Achievements of the 1960s

By 1960, the nation's foremost example of the multiversity included seven campuses and research stations up and down the state—the "thousand-mile university" as it was sometimes called. The whole enterprise cost $360 million a year to run, and the cost—like enrollment and everything else—was skyrocketing. As a complement to sheer size, however, the University now offered an enviable diversity of academic and cultural fare and opportunities for scientific and scholarly activity that could be matched by few other institutions.

In 1961 the Regents adopted a University Academic Plan outlining the needs of the future and emphasizing the theme of unity with diversity. There would be established in the next few years a new law school at Davis, engineering programs at Davis and Santa Barbara, medical schools at San Diego, Irvine, and Davis, a school of architecture at Los Angeles, and expanded health-sciences enrollments at both San Francisco and Los Angeles.

New general campuses at San Diego, Irvine, and Santa Cruz offered University planners a rare opportunity for innovation and experiment. As the first campuses to be designed from the start with a view to eventual high enrollments, they were encouraged to evolve along lines that would foster individuality yet at the same time meet the University's traditional standards of excellence.

Both San Diego and Santa Cruz adopted "cluster college" plans, a concept that would help reduce the feeling of institutional bigness while making the undergraduate educational experience more meaningful. Irvine, located in the most rapidly growing county in California, would emphasize the relation of campus to environment by offering strong programs in urban planning and environmental design.

In the first half-dozen years of President Kerr's administration, the knowledge explosion and society's efforts to keep abreast of it demanded more kinds of classes at higher instructional levels and a constantly growing range of research.

Ten new schools or colleges were created, along with eighty new programs leading to master's degrees and sixty-eight to the doctorate. Many of these advanced programs were established at Davis, Riverside, and Santa Barbara, and several were instituted at San Diego.

The Regents approved an important long-range plan guaranteeing access to outstanding research libraries for the new and smaller campuses. Berkeley and Los Angeles continued to develop their collections as primary research sources, while their card catalogs were given universitywide distribution.

This plan encouraged the smaller campuses, in addition to building up their basic libraries, to acquire collections unique within the University. Substantial economies were achieved by having the San Diego campus buy and catalog books, not only for its own new undergraduate library but, simultaneously, for those of Santa Cruz and Irvine.

Between 1958 and 1964, the University's instructional staff increased from 4,125 to 5,963; by 1970, it was 10,000. Every campus now claimed its share of luminaries. Both faculty and students were reflecting credit on their institution with a growing roster of honors.

The faculty included 15 Nobel Laureates, 121 members of the National Academy of Sciences, and 150 members of the

American Academy of Arts and Sciences. In addition, UC faculty members received a record 618 Guggenheim Fellowships between 1964 and 1970. Students ranked high in Woodrow Wilson and National Science Foundation Fellowships and in Fulbright Awards for study abroad.

Meanwhile, scholars were finding new opportunities for the development of special interests in the humanities. A universitywide Institute of Creative Arts was established, enabling a number of faculty members to devote substantial periods of time to creative activity.

Students were taking advantage of an opportunity rare in public higher education provided by an Education Abroad Program. The first overseas center was set up at the University of Bordeaux in 1962 and included 80 students. Today 3,600 UC students study at 141 institutions in 35 countries under the auspices of the program. Another estimated 2,300 UC students study abroad through other programs every year.

In the early 1960s, the Regents created a special scholarship program for outstanding students needing financial aid, and made available a number of tuition scholarships for exceptional students from other countries, thus supplementing programs that had been supported for many years by alumni and the state. The Regents also provided funds for the Educational Opportunity Program, established in 1964, to encourage enrollment of low-income and ethnic minority students—one of the earliest efforts of its kind in the nation.

During this period, the University accelerated and broadened its services to the people and government of California. Special institutes of governmental and public affairs at Berkeley, Los Angeles, and Davis were conducting research on metropolitan, state, and regional problems. University scientists continued to work toward solutions to such problems as smog control, water conservation and the desalinization of sea water, traffic and airport safety, sewage disposal, forestry conservation, and the assurance of adequate food for a growing population.

The demand for "lifelong learning" was reflected in the expansion of offerings by University Extension. A high proportion of the state's lawyers, dentists, and doctors were availing themselves of programs offered by Continuing Education of the Bar and Continuing Education in Medicine and the Health Sciences. Engineers, scientists, teachers, and business people—the majority holding at least one degree, and many with a master's or a doctorate—were returning to the classroom at intervals throughout their careers. Today University Extension serves 500,000 students a year.

Few California homes, professions, industries, farms, or human lives were not in some way served by the University. Though an institution still less than a century old, its impact upon society had become immense.

The Master Plan

California was growing—at a rate of 500,000 citizens a year—and so was the University. When Clark Kerr became President in 1958, UC had 47,000 students and was expected to enroll almost 130,000 by 1975. The state colleges and the community colleges would be adding even greater numbers.

Yet the unproductive competition in California higher education that President Sproul had contended with raged unabated, with no general agreement about how responsibilities would be divided for accommodating the imminent tidal wave of students. It was clear that if higher education did not respond quickly, the legislature, impelled by a growing sense of crisis, would act on its own.

In 1959, President Kerr proposed that the State Board of Education and the Regents meet jointly to launch a new planning study that would ensure access for students during the years of growth while avoiding costly duplication of effort within higher education. Soon thereafter, the legislature passed a resolution formally asking the State Board of Education and the University to work on a plan for the orderly expansion of California higher education in the decades ahead.

The result was the 1960 *Master Plan for Higher Education in California,* approved in principle by the Regents and the State Board in December 1959. Key portions of the Master Plan were enacted into law as the Donahoe Higher Education Act and signed by Governor Edmund G. Brown on April 14, 1960.

The Master Plan formalized the mission and pool of students for each of the three public segments of higher education—UC, the state colleges, and the community colleges. UC was to draw its undergraduates from the top one-eighth of California high school graduates and was given near-exclusive authority for doctoral and professional education and advanced research. The state colleges admitted their students from the top one-third of high school graduates and had responsibility for education through the master's degree. There was also a provision for offering joint doctorates with the University of California or an independent institution. The community colleges were to take any student over eighteen who could benefit from study and to offer vocational education and academic instruction through the first two years of college, including offering the opportunity to transfer to a four-year college or university.

The Master Plan reaffirmed California's commitment, forged during the Progressive era early in the century, to offer a place at a public college or university to every citizen with the talent and ambition to succeed. One measure of the Master Plan's success is that during the more than forty years since its approval the quality of the state's educational system, despite the pressures of growth, has not declined but risen.

As early as 1962, news of California's Master Plan attracted visitors from other countries seeking models for expanding their higher-education systems. A 1988 team of international visitors from the Organization for Economic Cooperation and Development observed that California had succeeded in encouraging "constructive competition and cooperation" among its colleges and universities, and praised the "complex of creativity" that makes the California system an exemplar for countries around the world.[15] The social, cultural, and economic advantages such a system has given California are enormous. Many of those advantages are a result of the Master Plan for Higher Education, which the legislature has periodically reviewed but never replaced.

Clark Kerr described the Master Plan as a structure for planning rather than a formal plan, a treaty among competing interests, and a vision of broad educational opportunity for a democratic, technological, and meritocratic society. In the simplicity and effectiveness with which it unites access and excellence, the Master Plan is also one of the great organizational ideas of twentieth-century higher education.

Decentralizing the University

The system of governance that President Kerr inherited in the late 1950s was clearly too cumbersome and slow moving for a university in the midst of a postwar boom, with seven campuses—and more in the offing—an enrollment of 50,000, and a growing and complex network of government-sponsored research. A wider sharing of authority was not just desirable but essential. With the support of the Regents, the chief campus officers, and the faculty, President Kerr initiated a reorganization that was to transform the University of California in far-reaching ways.

The animating principle of this reorganization was a major transfer of decision-making authority from the Regents and the President to the campuses—a revolution in governance that made the chancellorship, in Kerr's words, "the central locus of administration" in the University of California.[16] For the first time, Chancellors had broad authority over the day-to-day management of the campus; for the first time, they were in fact as well as in name chief executive officers, responsible for their campus's academic, physical, and fiscal plans.

Decentralization encouraged more efficient, more collaborative, and more locally relevant decision making. Just as important, it was a Copernican shift in governance that marked the future direction the University would take as a multi campus system—a federated union of research universities, each enjoying considerable autonomy and each seeking excellence in its own way, but unified by common standards for the admission of students, the appointment and promotion of faculty, and the approval of academic programs.

Student Unrest

The 1960s brought the coming of age of the huge Baby Boom generation; the passionate drive of minority groups for full citizenship; a prolonged, unpopular war in Vietnam; and years of political and social ferment. In an era of widespread social protest, the academic community would at times become the main vortex of events.

In the fall of 1964, the new era of student activism was dramatically inaugurated in a clash between Berkeley students and University authorities over on-campus volunteer recruitment and fund-raising for off-campus political activities, most involving civil rights. The ensuing controversy, known as the Free Speech Movement—the FSM—was led by an intense, cerebral philosophy student named Mario Savio. Although the spark that ignited the FSM was a dispute over the limits of political activity on campus, the movement's broader message of rebellion and social protest struck a responsive chord among thousands of students. As President Kerr himself had pointed out, for many of these students, the University—despite the exciting opportunities it offered—was a large and lonely place.

Before a crowd assembled in Sproul Plaza, Savio made the instructions on class computer enrollment cards—"Do not fold, bend, spindle, or mutilate"—the slogan of a generation. In another memorable metaphor, Savio urged students to "throw their bodies on the gears and the machinery" and bring the University to a halt.

The student revolt that began at Berkeley quickly spread, with varying intensity, to other UC campuses and ultimately to many other universities as well. Similar student movements broke out in Europe and Japan. Frequently, demonstra-

Antiwar demonstration at UCLA. Photograph courtesy UCLA Daily Bruin.

tions at UC and other American universities were triggered by off-campus causes—civil rights in the South, capital punishment, U.S. involvement in Southeast Asia, and others.

Widespread student unrest was an unprecedented and polarizing phenomenon in American higher education. Some saw the student movement as the front line of the fight for social justice; others saw it as a profoundly threatening repudiation of public order and the rule of law. Opinions were as divided within the University as in society at large. Disagreements within and beyond the UC community ripened into warfare as the University became *the* issue in the politics of the state.

As student protests over the war and other issues escalated, so did criticism of President Kerr, who quickly became the focus of public and legislative anger as campus turmoil dragged on. Some Regents were openly critical as well. Kerr was an internationally distinguished educator and had led the University during pivotal years in its history. Nonetheless, the Regents voted to dismiss him in January 1967, a little over two months after the election of Governor Ronald Reagan, who as a candidate had promised to "clean up the mess at Berkeley." Kerr's response was that he would be leaving the presidency as he came—"fired with enthusiasm."

The passage of time has brought new judgments and perspectives on the drama of student unrest. Clark Kerr, who went on to head the Carnegie Commission on Higher Education, was named President Emeritus by the Board of Regents in May 1974 and was hailed as "one of the giants of American education"; today he is recognized as among the most distinguished of the twentieth century's educational leaders.

And three decades after the Academic Senate voted to support the students in their conflict with Kerr and the Berkeley administration, the Berkeley campus dedicated the Sproul Hall steps—the stage from which Mario Savio delivered his fiery calls to dismantle the University—to his memory and to the spirit of the Free Speech Movement. One of the speakers at that dedication expressed the hope that "each generation of Berkeley students will produce its share of dissidents, rebels, and disturbers of the peace, that they will continue to provoke, that they will try the University's patience and tolerance. . . . The very health of this university, the very sanity and survival of our nation, depends on it."[17]

That is not the way it looked in the early months of 1967, when the University was without a president and close to a state of siege. Harry Wellman, a respected agriculturalist and administrator under Kerr, agreed to serve as Acting President for a year while the Regents searched for a new president.

Harry Wellman, Acting President, 1967. Photograph courtesy University Archives.

Their choice was Charles Johnston Hitch, a quiet, brilliant economist who had been a Rhodes scholar and, for thirteen years, an Oxford don. A leader in applying economic principles to problems of management, he founded the economics division of the RAND Corporation and, under Presidents Kennedy and Johnson, rationalized and revolutionized planning and budgeting at the Department of Defense. In 1965 Kerr had persuaded Hitch to leave the Department of Defense to take the job of Vice President for Finance and University Comptroller.

Hitch became the University's thirteenth President on January 1, 1968. In his inaugural address, he called on the University to bring its intellectual resources to bear on the plight of the nation's cities, whose long-festering problems of housing, transportation, pollution, crime, poverty, and discrimination had burst into public consciousness as a result of the urban riots earlier in the decade. Later he established an ambitious part-time degree program, called The Extended University, to put a UC education within the reach of working adults, older citizens, and other groups that traditional academic programs did not reach. Both initiatives, visionary and pioneering though they were, fell victim to budget cuts in Sacramento.

Hitch was more successful in his efforts to apply the planning principles he had first developed at RAND to managing the University. He reorganized the planning process to create, for the first time, explicit and consistent links between academic and budgetary planning.

But his two most important goals arose out of the conflicts of the time—to protect the University from both internal and external threats to its autonomy and academic freedom, and to start the process of healing the wounds inflicted by years of student dissent, particularly the divisions on the Board of Regents generated by differences over the handling of student protest and the firing of Clark Kerr.

Neither task proved easy. During the Hitch years (1968–75) campus turmoil rose to a crescendo in the struggle over People's Park, three acres of unused University-owned land near Berkeley's Telegraph Avenue that students and street people transformed into a community park in the spring of 1969. When the University put a chain-link fence around the property (which had been intended for much-needed student housing), rioting erupted. One person was killed and scores injured. Governor Reagan ordered the National Guard into Berkeley; over the next ten days, almost 1,000 people were arrested.

In the turbulent years from 1964 through the early 1970s, demonstrations and protests became a routine part of academic life. Incidents at Santa Barbara, San Diego, and UCLA were marked by violence and caused a growing rift between campuses and their communities. Students protested what they saw as the University's complicity in the war and its inaction on pressing social issues; faculty on just about every campus deadlocked in acrimonious debate; legislators demanded harsh action against rebellious students. As controversies piled up, public disenchantment with the University mushroomed. "I sometimes feel as if I am surrounded only by angry people," Hitch once sadly observed.

The Steady State

The student revolution was not the only problem Hitch and the University faced. With an unfriendly Governor in Sacramento and an economic slowdown in the state, in the late 1960s and early '70s the University's budgets went from bad to worse.

At the same time, the 1970 census data and projections of birth rates and immigration suggested that earlier estimates of continually expanding student enrollments into the 1980s and beyond were overly optimistic. University planning in the 1960s had assumed that enrollment on UC's eight general campuses would eventually go as high as 200,000, with campuses like Irvine, San Diego, and Santa Cruz ultimately topping out at 27,500 each.

In the early 1970s, new projections indicated that the rate of growth would be slower than anticipated and that the University was entering a "steady state." This meant a dramatic and sudden shift in focus from establishing new programs and

Charles J. Hitch,
President, 1968–75.
Photograph courtesy
University Archives.

facilities throughout the University system to developing the special academic strengths, approaches, and environments of each campus. The University's 1972 Growth Plan and its 1974 Academic Plan, which revised total projected enrollment significantly downward, defined these shifts in direction.

By the mid-1970s, the tide of student protest had subsided, and the University, despite its continuing budgetary stresses, was at last on an even keel. Hitch stepped down as President in July 1975, satisfied that the University had weathered the worst of its internal and external threats and that the Board of Regents was once again united. He was a thinker, a planner, and a man of reason in a passionate time, a leader whose honesty and directness had earned him the respect of even the University's harshest critics. Looking back, he said his most important contribution was "the preservation of the Master Plan and the freedom and autonomy which are its corollaries."[18] It was a remarkable accomplishment, achieved under punishingly difficult circumstances.

Planning for Hard Times

The problems the University confronted in the mid-1970s were less dramatic than those of the previous decade but no less challenging. A new Governor in Sacramento did not mean renewed support for UC; every year was a struggle. And the increasingly diverse ethnic and racial composition of California's population constituted a social and educational imperative that had to be addressed.

The new President of the University, David S. Saxon (1975–83), had a reputation for independence, integrity, and a strong vision of the University and its mission. As a young assistant professor of physics, Saxon was one of thirty-one UC faculty members who were dismissed in 1950 for refusing to sign the loyalty oath. When the oath was declared invalid two years later, Saxon returned to the physics department at UCLA and to a career marked by increasingly responsible academic and administrative posts, culminating in his selection as fourteenth President.

His agenda for the University was straightforward. What made the University of California unique, he said, was its "endemic excellence"—the high quality of its academic programs across large and small campuses alike. Not all campuses were at the same stage of development or the same level of distinction, but taken together they displayed a consistent academic strength that no other large multicampus system had ever achieved.

In an era marked by budget limitations and uncertain enrollments, Saxon argued, the University had a challenging twofold task: to maintain the "intellectual vitality and zest" of the mature campuses like Berkeley, UCLA, Davis, and San Francisco, while also ensuring that the University's traditional expectations of quality were met and extended at the younger and still-developing campuses at Irvine, Riverside, San Diego, Santa Barbara, and Santa Cruz. Three years into the Saxon administration, political developments in the state were to make that task even more challenging.

The Tax Revolt

In 1978, Californians approved Proposition 13, a ballot initiative that slashed property taxes—the traditional mainstay of counties and school districts—and froze property tax rates at the level they had been in 1975, capping future increases at two percent annually. Following Proposition 13's passage, property tax revenue plummeted between six and seven billion dollars a year, a sum equivalent to 40 percent of the revenues of all California counties combined.[19] As the state scrambled to help schools, cities, and counties make up some of the funding they had lost at the ballot box, it became clear that all publicly supported enterprises were at risk.

The University, Saxon told the Regents, must accelerate its planning for "an era of reallocation and consolidation."[20] While the University's planners would not shrink from considering a wide range of potential actions, from encouraging more intercampus cooperation to phasing out certain programs, Saxon made it clear that closing a campus—a topic of much speculation—would not be among them.

Besides the fiscal effects of tax-limiting initiatives, there was also the long-term demographic picture to consider. The data projected a decline of 15 percent in the number of eighteen-to twenty-four-year-olds by the early 1990s. Although Saxon believed that the University's quality would continue to make it attractive to students and thus mitigate the dimensions of this potential decline, he also recognized that without careful planning the impact on the University's fiscal and academic vitality could be devastating. He wanted, above all, to avoid a series of ad hoc, across-the-board cuts that treated all programs—the outstanding and the ordinary—alike. Given the unrelenting budgetary pressures and the downward enrollment projections, the only way the University could control its own future was by rigorously protecting the best of its academic programs.

At the urging of several Chancellors, Saxon also encouraged vigorous private fund-raising at the campuses and provided the smaller campuses with seed money for development activities. This initial investment has brought billions of dollars into the University in the years since.

The battle to sustain the University's quality in an era of waning public investment was waged throughout the Saxon administration. The success of Proposition 13 spawned a host of tax-cutting initiatives, among them Proposition 9, a 1980 ballot measure that proposed to halve the state income tax, at an estimated cost of $4.8 billion in its first year.[21] Given the public mood, the conventional wisdom went, any official who dared to oppose tax limitation was courting disaster. Saxon refused to be discouraged by this or by Proposition 9's enormous early lead in public opinion polls. He gave a series of speeches up and down the state documenting the harm the initiative would do to the University and other publicly funded activities; Saxon was one of only a handful of state leaders to speak out against it. In the end, Proposition 9 was defeated.

Bakke v. The Regents of the University of California

President Daniel Coit Gilman had said that the University of California was to be an institution "of the people and for the people" of this state. The civil rights movement of the 1960s had turned a powerful spotlight on the unequal access to education that curtailed the aspirations and opportunities of so many minority citizens. As the 1970s wore on, the state's changing demography vividly underscored the gap between the promise of Gilman's words and the reality of California society.

The University was overwhelmingly white, while California's minority population was growing by leaps and bounds: in 1977, 37 percent of the state's K–12 students were members of minority groups, a figure that was expected to rise to 56 percent by 1990.[22] A 1974 legislative resolution expressed the legislature's intent that both UC and CSU encompass in their student bodies the ethnic and racial composition of the graduating classes in California's high schools. But since black and Hispanic students qualified for the University at far lower rates than whites and Asians did, it was clear that major new strategies would be required to enroll such students at anything approaching their proportion in the population.

The University had long been exploring ways to diversify its student body, beginning with its 1964 Educational Opportunity Program, aimed at low-income and minority students. During Saxon's administration, UC redoubled its efforts. Experience had demonstrated the importance of motivating students early in their schooling, so the Partnership Program he initiated concentrated on working with junior high schools throughout the state, eventually becoming the largest program of its kind in the country.

The need for diversity in graduate and professional programs was equally compelling. UC's campuses experimented with a variety of approaches to enrolling more minority students, among them admissions programs that sought to broaden the evaluation of student qualifications to include measures of likely success in a field or profession beyond the traditional criteria of grades and test scores. These experiments at the graduate and professional level were inevitably susceptible to controversy because of the intense competition for spaces. The UC Davis Medical School, for example, received 3,737 applications for 100 places in 1974, the year in which a white student named Allan Bakke applied and was turned down. Bakke sued. The Davis program set aside a certain number of spaces for qualified minority students, a practice that Bakke's attorneys argued was unfair and discriminatory. The University ultimately appealed to the U.S. Supreme Court, thus making the UC Davis Medical School admissions program a national test case for the use of race and ethnicity in the admissions process.

In a divided 1978 ruling, the Supreme Court held that the Davis medical school special admissions program was invalid under the Constitution because it reserved to minority applicants places for which white students could not compete, a denial, in the Court's view, of equal protection. But it also ruled that race and ethnicity can be considered, as one factor among others, in the admissions process. In effect, the Court said, the Davis program's goal of enrolling a diverse student body served "a substantial [State] interest" and was legally valid, but the means it employed were not.

President Saxon immediately announced that admissions programs throughout the University would be scrutinized and, if necessary, brought in line with the guidelines set down by *Bakke*. And he also announced that the University would continue vigorously to seek out qualified women and minority students within the scope laid down by the Supreme Court.

Bakke was not the definitive ruling on race-sensitive admissions many had hoped for. But it did establish, as a matter of law, the legitimacy of diversity as an educational goal and the right of universities to consider race and ethnicity in their pursuit of that goal. It was to be almost twenty years before this principle became once again a subject of public dispute—from within the University itself.

New Intellectual Horizons

Despite fiscal, political, and legal challenges, the intellectual life of the University continued to thrive. During the 1970s a research team of UC San Francisco and Stanford University scientists developed recombinant DNA techniques and thereby set the stage for the biotechnological revolution. At UC San Diego, the Institute on Global Conflict and Cooperation was established to look beyond the weapons-oriented preoccupations of the Cold War and examine the broader issues that underlie global conflict.

And at the Lawrence Berkeley Laboratory, a young physicist named Jerry Nelson developed the first major innovation in telescope design since Isaac Newton's reflector telescope. A group of UC astronomers had come to David Saxon in 1977 with a proposal to use Nelson's design to build the world's largest optical telescope, an instrument that would shatter the limits imposed by all previous telescope technology. It was not a promising time for an enormously expensive venture in pure science dependent on radically new instrumentation. But

William H. Keck Observatory atop Mauna Kea in Hawai'i.
Photograph by Andrew Perala.

Saxon was convinced that astronomy and astrophysics were ripe for important advances and that the chance to build the first of an entirely new generation of telescopes was a unique opportunity the University should pursue. He encouraged the project despite the dismal prospects for funding. Saxon's successor, David Pierpont Gardner, was President by the time the University entered into a partnership with Cal Tech that ultimately resulted in not just one but two telescopes on Mauna Kea in Hawai'i, with funding from the W. M. Keck Foundation of Los Angeles.

Engineers at the Lawrence Berkeley Laboratory successfully executed Nelson's complex and revolutionary design—a series of thirty-six mirror segments, computer-adjusted every half-second to function as a single reflecting surface—and in the process created a tool so sensitive that a viewer looking through the telescope on Earth could see a candle on the moon. Today the twin Keck telescopes, the largest in history, are enabling researchers to do pioneering work in mapping galaxies, exploring the formation of solar systems, and finding answers to such fundamental questions as the origin and ultimate fate of the universe. The seed planted in lean times has borne spectacular fruit.

In 1982, the year before Saxon left office, the Conference Board of Associated Research Councils rated Berkeley's graduate programs first in the nation in all fields except the biological sciences—that distinction went to UCLA. UC San Diego and UC Santa Barbara were ranked among the universities whose graduate programs showed the most improvement. The University had added three new Nobel Prize winners to its roster since 1975. In spite of a series of draconian budgets, academic quality remained strong.

Yet the University had been damaged. Signs of difficulty in faculty recruitment were especially worrisome. Saxon's final message as President was that the University had gone as far as it could go in absorbing funding cuts; continuing fiscal erosion could precipitate an irreversible decline in quality. The University of California, he warned, was at a crossroads.

The Booming 1980s

The year 1983 brought the University a striking opportunity. The state's new Governor, George Deukmejian, was the first California chief executive in nearly two decades to make higher education a priority. The University's new President, David Pierpont Gardner, persuaded the Governor and the legislature to approve a 30 percent increase in UC's operating budget in his first year, the largest single increase in a state-funded UC budget in the University's history. It was a turning point for the struggling University. Among other things, Gardner's skill and success in making the case for University support during his first few years as President wiped out the 16 percent lag in faculty salaries between UC and the institutions with which it competed most vigorously for faculty.

David Gardner (1983–92) came to UC from the University of Utah, where he had been President for the previous ten years. He had a long history with the University of California, however, including service as a faculty member and Vice Chancellor at Santa Barbara during its period of greatest student turmoil. He had also served as a Vice President under Charles Hitch. Just before his selection as UC President he had co-chaired a national commission on K–12 public education whose April 1983 report, *A Nation at Risk,* galvanized the largest effort in a generation to raise the dismal performance of U.S. public schools. He was low-key in manner, precise in speech, analytical in his approach to problems, and impeccably prepared.

With the California economy emerging from its doldrums, the 1984–85 budget that Gardner successfully negotiated was the first of a series of strong budgets. Over the next six years UC established three new professional schools at San Diego, Riverside, and Santa Barbara; started major new research centers and initiatives, including the universitywide Humanities Research Institute at Irvine and the Center for German and European Studies at Berkeley; and expanded research into issues related to K–12 education. Steps to strengthen undergraduate teaching included a program of seminars for lower-division students and a major report on increasing the weight given to teaching in the University's faculty reward system. After a long drought of meager state capital funds, construction on UC campuses boomed: between 1983 and 1993 the

University's capital budget rose nearly fifteenfold, from $16.5 million to $240 million.

During the Gardner years, the University awarded its one-millionth degree, and five of its faculty members earned Nobel Prizes.

A Pacific Rim State

California, with its huge economy, its fast-growing multi-ethnic population, and its key location on a chain of nations stretching from Chile to Japan, was rapidly establishing itself as an international leader on the Pacific Rim. During the 1980s, the state was a favored destination for immigrants from the Pacific Rim, especially Mexico and Asia. Throughout much of the decade, California's annual population growth mounted to almost 600,000—the equivalent of the entire population of the state of Delaware.

Gardner saw the University as central to California's ability to realize its potential as a Pacific Rim state. Accordingly, under his leadership the University began a series of major initiatives to direct more of its teaching, research, and public service activities to helping California consolidate its leadership in the region.

UC's Education Abroad Program (EAP), focused predominantly on the nations of Europe since the establishment of its first study center at the University of Bordeaux in 1962, doubled the number of foreign institutions at which undergraduates could choose to study. Many of the new study centers were located in Pacific Rim countries such as Korea and the Philippines. Research burgeoned on issues related to Mexico, Central and Latin America, and Asia.

Among the most exciting of the Pacific Rim initiatives was

Education Abroad Program students in India. Photograph courtesy the Education Abroad Program.

UC San Diego's Graduate School of International Relations and Pacific Studies (IR/PS). At the time of its founding in 1986, IR/PS was the first new professional school established at the University of California in two decades. The school is unique among American international relations programs in its emphasis on the business, economics, and politics of the Pacific Rim. It quickly gained recognition for the excellence of its faculty and programs, and today it is internationally known for its research on the Asia Pacific region and its role in educating professionals skilled in the culture and commerce of this vital area of the world.

Growth Again

The 1980s did not usher in the precipitous decline in undergraduate enrollments UC planners of the previous decade had expected. On the contrary, for a variety of reasons ranging from the state's booming population to a surge in private university tuition that underscored what an educational bargain UC was, the campuses were flooded with applications from students eager for a UC education. As enrollments increased, the proportion of underrepresented minority students—blacks, Hispanics, and Native Americans—began to rise.

In the fall of 1988, President Gardner told the Regents that UC would need to accommodate an additional 63,000 students by 2005. To do so, it would need to build three new campuses.[23] The obvious choice of location for the first campus was the San Joaquin Valley, an expanding region in the heart of California that had been considered but not selected as a site for one of the new campuses built in the 1960s. The University took its message about impending growth to state leaders in Sacramento, arguing that expansion was necessary if UC was to serve California students in the future as it had in the past.

Conflicts and Controversies

There were, of course, problems as well as progress. The national movement against apartheid in the mid-1980s led to pressure on many organizations to divest themselves of stock in companies doing business in South Africa. UC students brought this matter to the forefront in 1985 and, at the request of student Regent Fred Gaines, the Board held a series of discussions on the pros and cons of the issue. President Gardner opposed divestment on the grounds that it would embroil the University in what was essentially a political issue and violate the Regents' fiduciary responsibility as trustees of UC's investments. In June 1985, the Regents adopted a plan proposed by President Gardner that would create a UC committee to monitor the University's investments in South Africa in terms of social responsibility.

The issue continued to generate discord, however. A year later, at the urging of Governor George Deukmejian, the Regents voted for divestment—a rare instance of the Board's dissenting from a Gardner position.

A second and later controversy involved the President himself. Gardner announced in November 1991 that he would step down the following October, a decision precipitated by the recent death of his wife. At the time of his announcement the California economy had entered one of its cyclical downturns, and the generous UC budgets of earlier years had evaporated. To help UC attract and retain skilled administrators despite its budget constraints, the Regents had approved the awarding of deferred compensation and a supplemental retirement annuity to certain UC executives, including the President, as long as they remained with the University for a specific period of time. President Gardner's planned retirement date would have made him ineligible for these benefits, but in recognition of his contributions and the special circumstances of his decision to retire, the Board voted to waive the vesting date and award him both deferred compensation and supplemental retirement funds.

In a period of cutbacks and early retirement programs, the Board's decision became the subject of heated controversy when it was made public. Months of sensationalized press accounts of alleged administrative overspending, excessive executive salaries and perquisites, and lax Regental oversight shredded the University's image in Sacramento and among the public.

President Gardner retired on October 1, 1992. His final months in office were shadowed by dissension and criticism, despite the great strides the University had made under his leadership. The most significant of these was the rebuilding of the University's fiscal foundation—an accomplishment that was crucial to the University's success in sustaining its academic quality through the hard times that lay ahead.

The University under Fire

For the next several years it seemed as if the University could not escape the headlines; one media tempest followed another. Most centered on administrative salaries and spending in the Office of the President, but others were sparked by incidents on the campuses—irregularities in fund-raising by campus foundations, disputes at two campuses over the Chancellors' leadership, and even a legislative outcry over the appointment of 1960s activist Angela Davis, now a UC faculty member, to an endowed professorship at Santa Cruz.

The most notorious incident, however, involved a teleconferenced meeting of the President's Council of Chancellors in March 1994. On that occasion, the President and several Chancellors, in a private conversation before the meeting began, roundly criticized legislators who had recently turned down the appointment of a nominee for the Board of Regents. Unbeknownst to the speakers, their remarks were being recorded on audiotape. Verbatim portions of the conversation appeared in a San Francisco newspaper several weeks later.

The result, predictably, was legislative outrage and a university once again on the defensive.

A New President and an Economic Crisis

The President who presided at that meeting, J. W. Peltason (1992–95), had been among the founding faculty and administrators at UC Irvine. Peltason left Irvine to accept the post of Chancellor of the University of Illinois–Champaign-Urbana in 1967 but accepted the invitation to become Irvine's second Chancellor in 1984, after a career that included seven years as head of the American Council on Education. He was a widely respected and nationally known figure in higher education as well as a seasoned administrator thoroughly familiar with the UC system.

He was noted for his insight, equanimity, and good humor, qualities he often had occasion to summon in his new post. In addition to enduring unrelenting newspaper attacks and embarrassing revelations about University management, he inherited a budget crisis of mammoth proportions. "I knew the Regents wanted me to hit the ground running," he said at his first Regents' meeting as President, "but I didn't know they meant running and ducking."

The good times of the 1980s had masked some serious structural problems, both in the California economy and in the state budget process. The end of the Cold War had spelled the end of California's military-based industries, a bitter blow to the economy. The state, accustomed to brief recessions and quick recoveries, found itself mired in a seemingly endless downturn. It was, in fact, the worst economic slump since the Great Depression.

And Proposition 13 and its aftermath—including Proposi-

tion 98, which was passed in 1988 and required that 40 percent of the annual state budget be allocated to the K–12
schools and the Community Colleges—had not only shrunk
revenues but also drastically curtailed the Governor's and the
legislature's ability to control the state budget. By the early
1990s, 85 percent of the state budget was already allocated
before a single decision about spending could be made, as a
result of various initiatives, statutes, and mandatory spending requirements. UC, along with the California State University, was locked into that unprotected 15 percent of state
programs.

Between 1990–91 and 1993–94, the University's cumulative
budget shortfall—the difference between what it would have
gotten under normal circumstances and what it actually
received—came to nearly a billion dollars. The measures UC
took to deal with this staggering gap in its state-funded budget included three early retirement programs, cutbacks in
administration, deferred salary increases—in one year, salaries
were cut—and higher student fees.

One apparent casualty of the state's plunge into fiscal crisis was the proposed tenth campus. The University's arguments to state officials about the need for three new UC campuses had largely fallen on deaf ears in 1988 and 1989; portents
of economic trouble were already in the air. The University,
however, had gone ahead with plans to select a site for a tenth
campus in the San Joaquin Valley, and in 1995 the Regents
voted to accept a gift of more than 7,000 acres near Merced's
Lake Yosemite from the Virginia Smith Trust. The next step—
an expensive one—was environmental planning for the new
campus. Peltason reluctantly concluded that there was no
point in going forward with environmental impact reports
when there was no money to build the campus.

Four Presidents: David S. Saxon (1975–83), David P. Gardner (1983–92),
J. W. Peltason (1992–95), and Richard C. Atkinson (1995–2003).
Photograph by Peg Skorpinski.

To his surprise, he was summoned to Sacramento by legislative leaders who demanded to know why the University's
plans were being delayed. He explained that the environmental impact reports would cost a million and a half dollars, and that was just the beginning. The legislature would
see that the University got its one and a half million, he was
told, if he agreed to go ahead with the EIRs; if he refused, the
penalty would be the loss of a planned $50 million budget
allocation to support UC faculty salaries. Since UC enthusi-
astically supported the much-needed campus and desperate-
ly needed the funds for faculty salaries, Peltason's response was
instantaneous: "You've found my price—fifty-one and a half
million dollars." Plans for the tenth campus proceeded.

Shortly after becoming President in October 1992, Peltason
announced a program of four initiatives to protect the University's quality. The most significant was a long-range plan-

ning initiative intended to cushion the University against wide swings in state funding despite California's fiscal problems and its convoluted budget process. Although a solution to budgetary gridlock did not emerge from this effort, something vitally important to the University did.

UC officials told Governor Pete Wilson that the University's survival as one of the world's great academic institutions required an end to the steep budgetary slide of the previous few years. A floor under the University's budget, they argued, would allow UC to plan for the future with some confidence instead of struggling from crisis to crisis. The Governor was convinced. He agreed to a compact with the University under which UC was promised a certain level of funding over the next four years, beginning in 1995. After years of fiscal free-fall, the University had at last gained a stable footing.

The Debate over Admissions

As early as 1987, President David Gardner warned that the legislature's 1974 resolution urging UC to achieve a student body that approximated the demography of California was on a collision course with the University's admissions policies as defined by the Master Plan.

Under the Master Plan, UC was to limit the students it admitted to the top 12.5 percent of California high school graduates statewide. Under the legislative resolution, UC's student body was to approximate the racial and ethnic make-up of California high school graduates statewide. The problem was that the different groups making up the 12.5 percent pool qualified for the University at very different rates. In the late 1980s, Asian students qualified for UC at a rate of about 26 percent, whites at 15 percent; Hispanics at around 5 percent, and blacks at 3.6 percent. UC's affirmative action programs had been established to address these disparities in eligibility that made some groups "underrepresented" in the University. California was now the most diverse state in the nation, a reality that lent added urgency to bringing more underrepresented students into higher education.

As Gardner explained to the Regents at their November 1987 meeting, the combination of growing numbers of UC applicants and wide gaps in eligibility meant that competing social and educational values had somehow to be reconciled. If UC's admissions policies favored students with the highest grades and test scores, the overwhelming majority selected would be white or Asian; if it continued to supplement grades and test scores with consideration of qualifications such as special talents or breadth of extracurricular activities, more underrepresented students, but fewer whites and Asians, would be selected. The University's mandated admissions pool of the top one-eighth of California high school graduates constituted a zero-sum game: whenever the representation of one racial or ethnic group went up, the representation of another inevitably went down.

The University, like colleges and universities nationwide, sought to strike a balance in its policies to assemble an entering class that included not just students with straight-A records, not just students who brought racial and ethnic diversity, but also students who reflected a variety of incomes and interests, as well as geographical diversity. Further, all eligible California students were guaranteed a place at the University, though not necessarily on their campus of first choice. But as long as demand for a UC education continued to be strong, especially demand for campuses—such as Berkeley and UCLA—that did not have room for every student who wanted to attend, the University's admissions policies would remain a target.

"I can't think of any policy issue either more sensitive, more politically complicated, more socially difficult to deal with," Gardner concluded, "[or] issues . . . more important in the long run to the University of California and, in fact, to relationships among and between the citizens of our state."[24]

It was a prescient remark. By the mid-1990s, the thirty-year social consensus supporting affirmative action in university admissions was beginning to fray. In 1993 and 1994, Mr. and Mrs. Jerry Cook of San Diego protested to a number of UC Regents and officials that their son, James, had been passed over for admission to UC San Diego's medical school while minority students with lower grades and test scores were admitted. (James Cook was accepted at UC Davis's medical school, which twenty years earlier had precipitated the *Bakke* case by denying admission to white applicant Allan Bakke.) The Cooks' charges led some Regents to call on the Board to abolish affirmative action; the President responded with a decision to present to the Regents a review of the University's affirmative action policies in admissions and employment. Ward Connerly, one of the Regents who requested this review, was explicit about his reservations regarding affirmative action and his intention to call for a vote on the issue at the Board's June 1995 meeting.

The stage was set for what became a prolonged and polarizing debate on the merits of affirmative action. As had been the case with divestment a decade earlier, the question before the Board was a controversial national and political issue. Like that earlier debate, this one included charges of political interference on the part of the state's Governor. Governor Wilson was running for President, and ending affirmative action was the centerpiece of his campaign.

Unlike divestment, however, this debate went straight to the heart of the University of California's role as a public university. Were its admissions policies fundamentally fair? In distributing educational opportunity, what were its responsibilities to students and to society in a state undergoing profound demographic change?

The administration's defense of its affirmative action programs, marshaled in a series of presentations to the Board from January to June 1995, persuaded some Regents of the soundness of UC's policies. But it aroused skepticism in others, who were inclined to doubt the reliability of some of the information the administration provided and regarded the President's pleas for more time to study the issue as a strategy for delay. As the months passed and it became clear that Regent Connerly would make good on his promise to bring the matter to a vote, various UC constituencies—among them the President, the Chancellors, and the Academic Senate—went on record supporting affirmative action as vital to the University's mission.

In July 1995, at a long and media-blitzed meeting interrupted by a bomb threat, the Regents voted to end consideration of race, gender, and ethnicity in admissions and employment and purchasing at the University of California. Governor Wilson led the fight on behalf of Regent Connerly's two resolutions—SP-1, on admissions, and SP-2, on employment and purchasing. During the course of the meeting the Regents heard from a long list of advocates, including the Reverend Jesse Jackson—also a U.S. presidential candidate—former speaker of the California Assembly Willie Brown, and one of their own number, Regent Roy Brophy, who left the Regents' table to speak as a private citizen and in that capacity warn his colleagues about the dangers attendant on passage of SP-1 and SP-2. President Peltason argued, to no avail, that the Board should at least postpone action until the following year. At that time a ballot initiative, Proposition 209, would allow the state's citizens to decide whether affirmative action should be abolished throughout all state agencies.

When the final vote came, it was a close one. SP-1 was approved by a margin of 14 to 10, with one abstention; SP-2, by 15 to 10.

Passage of SP-1 committed UC to the task of enrolling more minority students on its campuses without considering either race or ethnicity in selecting them. Virtually overnight, the University of California—which had been one of the first in the nation to establish affirmative action programs and had argued the *Bakke* case up to the Supreme Court—found itself a leader among American universities in dismantling race-attentive admissions.

Rankings

With the funding compact with the Governor in place, President Peltason's most important goal had been achieved. He had brought the University through three of the worst budget years in its history, all the while addressing its problems with an integrity and warm humanity that won UC many friends. He retired in October 1995, telling the Regents in his farewell remarks that the University had done far more than survive the dire years of the early 1990s. In the academic domain, he said, "the University of California has few equals and no superiors."

His judgment was validated that same month by the Na-

Supercomputer Center, UC San Diego.
Photograph by Kevin Walsh, UCSD Media Group.

tional Research Council (NRC), the research arm of the National Academy of Sciences. The NRC's comprehensive study of Ph.D. programs in American universities rated Berkeley first in the nation, San Diego tenth, and UCLA twelfth (the other nine universities in the top twelve were all private institutions). Most remarkable were UC's rankings as a system—more than half of its 229 graduate programs evaluated by the NRC were in the top twenty in the nation.[25] As if to echo this testimony to the University's distinction, three Nobel Prizes went to UC faculty members in October as well.

Two years later, an analysis of faculty research achievements at more than 200 U.S. institutions—*The Rise of American Research Universities*—gave the University equally glowing reviews, emphasizing the academic quality to be found across its nine campuses. All included departments and programs of

Paintings by Hans Hofmann, UC Berkeley Art Museum.
Photograph by Ben Ailes.

national or international stature; Santa Barbara, Riverside, and Santa Cruz were cited for the "astonishing" speed with which they had risen to national rank among research universities.[26] The philosophy of cultivating nine different but high-quality research universities—what David Saxon defined as "endemic excellence"—had created something new in the world of higher education: a great public university whose distinction is not limited to one or two flagship campuses but is genuinely universitywide. The University of California had come of age as a multicampus system.

Research and Economic Growth

In early 1996 it was apparent that the California economy was pulling out of its tailspin and beginning a steady climb in job creation and productivity. A major reason for the state's returning prosperity was its high-technology industries, among them computers, software, and information technology, which were fed by basic research conducted in the state's research universities.

President Richard C. Atkinson (1995–2003) viewed the California comeback as symptomatic of a shift in the economy toward reliance on knowledge as an engine of economic growth. He had begun his academic career in the late 1950s as a faculty member at Stanford University, where his teaching and research focused on the nature of human memory and cognition. The seminal importance of his scientific contributions was recognized by his election to the National Academy of Sciences at an early age.

One of the colleagues he worked with and admired at Stanford was its renowned dean of engineering, Frederick Terman. Terman had made economic history by spurring the industry-university cross-fertilization that created Silicon Valley. As a young faculty member, Atkinson saw firsthand the tremendous potential of the kind of bridge-building with industry that Terman had advocated with such tangible success.

As Chancellor of UC San Diego from 1980 to 1995, Atkinson pursued a strategy shaped by his Stanford experience and his years as Director of the National Science Foundation in the late 1970s. He encouraged technology transfer and active involvement with industry, especially with the small high-technology firms that were emerging in San Diego. He concentrated on faculty quality, on establishing a school of engineering, and on expanding the campus's ability to do cutting-edge research.

By the end of the 1980s, UC San Diego had become a dynamic factor in the region's economy, particularly in its recovery from a devastating recession caused by the demise of San Diego's defense-related industries. The role of UC San Diego was so clearly crucial that the area's revitalization in the early 1990s was described as "the Atkinson miracle."

President Atkinson believed that the University could and

must play a similar role for California. The Industry-University Cooperative Research Program, established early in 1996, focuses on stimulating innovation in the most promising areas for future economic growth—among them biotechnology, digital media, and microelectronics—through joint projects involving industry and UC researchers.

To produce the technically skilled workforce California's innovative economy demands, Atkinson committed UC to expanding enrollments in engineering and computer science by 50 percent by 2005. By 2002, the University had already exceeded this goal.

Governor Gray Davis was an enthusiastic advocate of the idea that investing in scientific innovation, and in the educated people who make it happen, is crucial to California's current and future prosperity. In 2000, he proposed the establishment of four California Institutes for Science and Innovation on UC campuses. The Institutes are charged with conducting sophisticated multidisciplinary research in areas critical to the state's economy, including nanoscience, telecommunications, information technology, and biomedicine, with California's high-technology businesses contributing nearly three dollars for every one invested by the state. A second, equally important mission is educating future scientific and entrepreneurial leaders by giving graduate students the opportunity to work on large and challenging problems with the state's best minds. The ultimate goal of the California Institutes is to lay the foundation for the economy of the future.

The Institutes embodied aspirations that were typically Californian in their optimism and ambitious scope. Yet efforts to expand research ties with the private sector were not universally welcomed, despite their roots in the University's land-grant tradition. Some within and outside the University pointed to the risk of skewing faculty research agendas or compromising the unfettered search for knowledge. In recent years University officials have sought to reshape UC policies to take these concerns into account and to accommodate new forms of industry-university relationships.

The growing demands on UC as a generator of knowledge are symptomatic of the distance between the remote pioneer outpost that California was in the nineteenth century and the technologically driven society it has become in the twenty-first. One-fifth of the nation's research and development is carried out in California's universities, nonprofit research institutions, and businesses, even though the state has only 12 percent of the nation's population. Its entrepreneurial energies and climate of opportunity have made this state the globe's fifth-largest economy, dependent on a constant supply of scientific and technological innovation. As the source of basic research and educated people, the University has become more central to society than ever before.

New Directions for Outreach

President Atkinson's goals for the University went far beyond strengthening its contributions to the California economy. At the top of his list was maintaining faculty quality: a distinguished faculty is an indispensable prerequisite to a great university. Next was ensuring the diversity of the University community in the post–affirmative action era, and in particular the diversity of its student body.

When the Regents voted to end consideration of race and gender in admissions in July 1995, they made it clear that diversity remained a priority on the University's agenda. SP-1

Healthy twins delivered at the UC San Francisco Medical
Center with the help of in vitro techniques.
Photograph by Mikkel Aaland.

declared that diversity was an "asset," and that "this policy will achieve a UC population that reflects this state's diversity through the preparation and empowerment of all students . . . to succeed rather than through a system of artificial preferences."

The administration and the Academic Senate faced two urgent tasks. The first was to revise the University's admissions policies and practices to reflect the new approach outlined in SP-1. Once accomplished, these changes became effective in fall 1997 for graduate students and spring 1998 for undergraduates.

The second was to create a strategy for expanding the University's outreach activities with the K–12 public schools. California's schools, once among the best in the nation, were now among the most troubled, particularly in urban areas. Despite strong public support, funding never seemed to keep up with the explosive growth of the school system and its steadily rising needs for teachers, classrooms, and textbooks.

Decades of sweeping demographic change meant that a majority of the schools' nearly six million students were now Latinos, African Americans, Asians, and other minorities. About one-fifth of K–12 students had limited proficiency in English; while most of these students were Spanish speaking, some fifty languages other than English were represented in classrooms across the state. Schools serving low-income and otherwise disadvantaged students tended to offer the fewest honors courses needed by students planning to attend UC. A teacher shortage of epic dimensions meant that thousands of students (including disproportionate numbers of disadvantaged students) were learning basic subjects, including mathematics and science, from teachers who had not majored in those disciplines. Many of these teachers lacked credentials and were teaching with emergency permits.

President Peltason had cautioned about the dangers of trying to sustain "a great university on the foundation of a crumbling school system." And now that race and gender were barred from consideration in the admissions process, helping to address the crisis in the K–12 schools was no longer just an institutional obligation but a compelling institutional necessity.

UC's partnership with the schools dated back to its earliest days; by the 1990s the campuses and the Office of the President were engaged in more than 800 cooperative programs with the public school system. In its 1997 report, an outreach task force mandated by SP-1 recommended a massive expansion of UC's partnerships with the K–12 schools and the

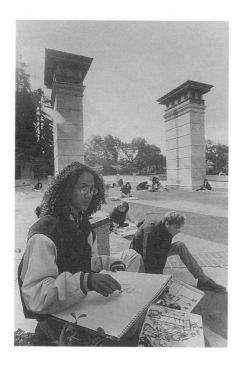

Landscape design students sketching on the Berkeley campus. Photograph by Peg Skorpinski.

Community Colleges, especially with those schools that historically had sent few students to the University. Noting that "it is through the schools . . . that UC can have the most powerful influence in equalizing educational opportunity," the task force estimated that real progress would require doubling, over five years, the University's annual $60 million investment in outreach to $120 million.[27]

Within a few years, spending on outreach had leaped beyond that five-year goal. In 2001 UC was spending more than $300 million a year on tutoring, mentoring, and counseling for K–12 students; partnerships with disadvantaged schools to improve curricula and instruction; opportunities for teachers to improve their skills; and programs to boost the number of Community College students transferring to the University.

Tidal Wave II and New Approaches to Admission

As the new century opened, demand for the University showed no signs of diminishing. UC was inundated with 92,000 freshman and transfer applications for 39,000 places in fall 2001. In the years between 2000 and 2010, it would need to grow by more than 50,000 students—5,000 students annually—to accommodate Tidal Wave II, the children of the Baby Boomers who would be seeking a UC education. And it would need to grow at an even faster annual rate and over a longer period of time than it had during the first tidal wave in the 1960s and 1970s. Such rapid expansion posed real challenges for the University, including the need to recruit some 7,000 new faculty members over that same decade without compromising UC's high standards of quality.

Inevitably, the stresses of expansion focused even more attention on the University's admissions policies and practices. Given that demand for places at most campuses exceeded supply, the means UC employed to select students would attract increasingly intense public and legislative scrutiny. It was imperative for the University to see that its admissions policies were, in President Atkinson's words, "demonstrably inclusive and fair."

"We should do this," President Atkinson stated, "by assessing students in their full complexity, which means considering not only grades and test scores but also what students have made of their 'opportunities-to-learn,' the obstacles they have overcome, and the special talents they possess."[28] In pursuit of this goal the President proposed, and the Academic

Senate and the Regents approved, several new approaches to admissions.

At the heart of these proposals was an effort to reconcile the University's traditionally high expectations of students with the realities of intense competition for admission, burgeoning cultural and social diversity, and the dramatically different learning opportunities available to California's young people. Their effect was twofold: to open up new avenues to the University, and to move it away from quantitative admissions formulas and closer to the kind of broad assessment of students' abilities and accomplishments practiced in selective private universities.

Achievement versus Aptitude

In February 2001, during his keynote address at the annual meeting of the American Council on Education, President Atkinson announced that he had asked the Academic Senate of the University of California to consider eliminating the SAT I aptitude test as a requirement for admission to UC. The overemphasis on the SAT and test scores, he went on to say, had created "the educational equivalent of a nuclear arms race" in which "anyone or any institution opting out of the competition does so at considerable risk." [29]

His announcement that the nation's largest user of the SAT might abandon the test had an immediate and electrifying impact on American higher education. A virtual rite of passage in the United States, the SAT is required for admission to most of the country's elite universities, and about two million high school students take it every year.

Some were quick to speculate that President Atkinson's motivation was to make it easier for underrepresented minority students to qualify for the University, since Latinos, African Americans, and Native Americans tended to do less well on the SAT than did whites and Asians. In reality, his reasons had far more to do with his skepticism about the soundness of any test that purported to measure innate mental abilities. As a cognitive scientist, he had long doubted the efficacy of such tests and had stated his reservations publicly on a number of occasions.

A democratic society, he argued, should judge students on what they had actually accomplished, not on "ill-defined notions of aptitude." He proposed that the University should instead employ achievement tests, tied to the college-preparatory curriculum, that measured the knowledge students had acquired during their schooling. Achievement tests, he asserted, are fairer to students, less vulnerable to charges of cultural or socioeconomic bias, and more appropriate for students and schools because they clarify what is important for students to learn.

In June 2002 the College Board, sponsor of the SAT, announced that beginning in 2005 it would align the test to the college-preparatory curriculum, adding a written essay and a more rigorous mathematics section to the seventy-six-year-old SAT. Atkinson welcomed the decision and praised the College Board for having "laid the foundation for a new test that will better serve our students and schools."

Transitions

President Atkinson announced in November 2002 that he would step down the following year. In addition to making the University more responsive to the economic needs of the state, he had presided over a historic transformation of the

University's processes for selecting students, hewing a careful and exacting path through a maze of clashing regental, faculty, and public views. In May 2001, with Atkinson's support, the Regents voted unanimously to rescind SP-1. The Board affirmed the University's intent to continue complying with Proposition 209 as well as its commitment to enrolling a student body that reflects both exceptional achievement and "the broad diversity of backgrounds characteristic of California."

UC posted some of the largest budget increases in its history during his presidency, and annual private giving exceeded a billion dollars for the first time. President Atkinson used the opportunities of prosperity to urge the University in innovative directions. UC extended its presence abroad with the establishment of California House, a center for UC activities in London, and plans for a Casa de California in Mexico City—one of many efforts to strengthen ties with Mexico. A new degree program—the Master of Advanced Study—offers working adults the chance to earn degrees in selected fields through University Extension.

President Atkinson was particularly concerned about embracing the opportunities offered by new technologies. In 1997, he established the California Digital Library (CDL), which today is unmatched in the scope and sophistication of its digital collections. The CDL is a leader in encouraging new forms of scholarly communication.

In the late 1990s the University was instrumental in creating Internet2, a national consortium of universities and industries to build high-speed computer networks that will advance teaching, scholarship, and research. The first Internet2 link between major universities in California and Mexico was forged in 2001 through a memorandum of understanding between the University and Mexican higher education leaders.

Toward the end of the Atkinson administration, recessionary storms that had been gathering nationwide hit California with spectacular force. In late 2002 government analysts in Sacramento were projecting a staggering $35 billion shortfall over the next eighteen months—more than twice California's budget deficit in the early 1990s. As one of a handful of state programs whose funding was unprotected by statute or mandatory spending requirements, the University was particularly vulnerable.

To deal with the fiscal crisis, the University instituted large cuts in areas ranging from administration to research. Student fees, which UC had held steady for seven years in a row, had leaped 40 percent by 2003. That same year the state's contribution to the University's outreach programs and professional development activities for K–12 teachers sank to one-fifth of what it had been at its height a few years earlier—a particularly painful reduction given the promise of these programs and the magnitude of the need. Moreover, few considered it likely that the state's fiscal troubles could be quickly resolved. The prospect of even deeper cuts remained—including curbing enrollments despite unprecedented student demand for a place at UC.

Clearly, the University's ability to sustain both its access and its excellence would be tested.

On June 11, 2003, the Regents chose Robert C. Dynes, Chancellor of UC San Diego, as the University's eighteenth President. Dynes, an expert on semiconductors and superconductors and a member of the National Academy of Sciences, spent twenty-two years in the private sector—at AT&T Bell Labo-

Robert C. Dynes,
President, 2003–.
Photograph courtesy
UC San Diego.

ratories—before joining the faculty at UC San Diego in 1991. He did so, he said, because he saw "that the locus of American innovation was shifting from industry to the academy."

During his seven years as UCSD Chancellor, Dynes was known for his egalitarian and energetic style. He guided the campus through a 25 percent growth in enrollment and the establishment of a school of management, a school of pharmacy and pharmaceutical sciences, and a new undergraduate college, as well as a public charter school on the campus dedicated to preparing low-income students for a university education.

On the occasion of his appointment as President, Dynes told the Regents that he recognized the pressures facing the University to accommodate large numbers of students despite shrinking public support. "There is a national consensus that American public universities must redefine how they deliver quality higher education," he said. "And the rest of the country is looking to the University of California to lead the way."

The University Past and Present

In the early days of statehood, the University served not only as a source of education but as a path to distinction for individuals in a new society that had few status-granting authorities. Later, it fed California's growing regionalism by establishing campuses in developing areas of the state: the struggle that ended with UCLA's taking its place as an equal alongside Berkeley was one skirmish in the long battle between the established, settled north and the youthful, exploding south.

And from early on in the state's history, the University's education, research, and service have been responsible in major ways for California's emergence as an international economic and cultural leader. Conversely, California's citizens have given the University the monetary and political support to create one of the most exciting and innovative centers of learning in the world. All of which is to say that the story of the University is the story of California itself.

The University of California today enrolls 200,000 students and employs 160,000 faculty and staff. UC encompasses ten campuses, five medical schools and teaching hospitals, three law schools, and more than 600 research centers, institutes, and programs. Its research and extension facilities span and crisscross the State of California, from a peak in the Sierra Nevada (the White Mountain Research Station) to below sea level in the Imperial Valley (an agricultural field station).

UC's more than 100 libraries house some thirty million volumes and are surpassed in size on the American continent only by the Library of Congress.

Graduate student examining seal at the Joseph M. Long Marine Laboratory, UC Santa Cruz. Photograph by Don Kenny.

No university or university system has such a major share of research dollars coming from the federal government, and private giving to UC exceeds that of any nonprofit institution except the Salvation Army. Its annual budget of $13 billion is larger than that of many states.

But what is really important about the University lies beyond the reach of numbers. The University of California is the product of three distinctive dreams, whose power has moved Californians to support it despite its occasional lapses and inevitable flaws. The first, brought west by New Englanders like Henry Durant, was the dream of a liberal education. The second was the dream of the university as an active force in society's problems and progress, symbolized by the Morrill Land-Grant College Act of 1862. The third is the dream of universal access, which binds the University to its sister segments, the California State University and the Community Colleges, in a commitment to the fullest possible realization of individual talent.

These dreams are the material out of which the University invented itself—and has sometimes been forced to reinvent itself as California has grown and changed. They have created that rarest of institutions, a public university of outstanding academic quality devoted to balancing a broad liberal education with highly specialized research.

Nothing could be more American—or more Californian—than the expectation that a UC Berkeley or a UC San Diego could be the equal of a Harvard or a Cambridge. Yet it is easy to forget what a bold assumption this is, and how profound its consequences have been.

University of California Campuses

« « «   » » »

BERKELEY

UC Berkeley was a founding member in 1900 of the Association of American Universities, established to advance the quality and standing of American doctoral institutions. In the century since then, the University's oldest campus has soared to the pinnacle of American higher education by just about any measure. Its faculty includes 127 members of the National Academy of Sciences, 101 members of the National Academy of Engineering, 18 Nobel Prize winners, and a U.S. Poet Laureate. UCB's nine-million-volume library is among the largest in the United States. Eighty museums, from the Phoebe Hearst Museum of Anthropology to the Museum of Vertebrate Zoology, house collections in a wide range of disciplines.

UC Berkeley's 29,000 students can choose from among 103 undergraduate programs, and the campus offers 163 graduate and 45 professional degrees. Student life is lively and varied, with many opportunities for undergraduates to become involved in exciting research with Berkeley's internationally distinguished faculty through the Undergraduate Research Apprentice Program and other activities. UC Berkeley's alumni have been leaders in every profession and in every walk of life.

Reflecting Pool in Memorial Glade. Photograph by Alan Nyiri.

DAVIS

Although next door to Sacramento and within easy reach of the San Francisco Bay Area, Davis takes pride in its small-town ambience; the bicycle is ubiquitous in this friendly and close-knit university community. Davis combines a distinguished faculty and excellent facilities for teaching and research.

Established as the University Farm in 1905, Davis was organized as a branch of the College of Agriculture in 1922. A School of Veterinary Medicine opened in 1948 and the College of Letters and Science in 1951. Eight years later, Davis was authorized as a general campus of the University. The School of Law held its first classes in 1966, followed by the School of Medicine in 1968 and the Graduate School of Management in 1981.

While continuing to be one of the world's leading centers for agricultural, biological, and environmental teaching and research, UCD in recent years has also won high praise for its offerings in the arts, humanities, social sciences, and the professions. The campus's academic quality was formally recognized in 1996 with an invitation to join the prestigious Association of American Universities.

Meyer Hall Atrium, UC Davis. Photograph by Alan Nyiri.

The cultural diversity of the campus is enriched by the presence of many students from foreign countries. Davis's devotion to teaching is reflected in its $30,000 Prize for Teaching and Scholarly Achievement, believed to be the largest award of its kind in the country.

Among Davis's off-campus facilities are the Lake Tahoe Center for Environmental Research, the Veterinary Medicine Teaching and Research Center in Tulare, the Bodega Marine Laboratory on the Pacific Ocean at Bodega Bay, the College of Engineering's applied science department at the Lawrence Livermore National Laboratory, and the UC Davis Medical Center in Sacramento. The Medical Center, essential to health care in the Sacramento area, has achieved special recognition for trauma care and for the most extensive telemedicine network in the country. The Center has been long recognized for its excellence in training family practitioners.

IRVINE

The Irvine campus opened in the fall of 1965 on 1,510 acres of Orange County ranch land three miles from the Pacific Ocean. The architect for the site, William Pereira, designed the campus as a series of concentric rings with a park at its center. In his architectural plan, Pereira saw UCI as the heart of a "city of intellect" that would grow with the surrounding community.

Founding Chancellor Daniel G. Aldrich Jr. envisioned Irvine as a land-grant university for the twenty-first century, expanding the agricultural mandate of the land-grant era into new forms of service for an urban society. UCI's pioneering School of Social Ecology, for example, is now a national model for interdisciplinary education and research focused on community problem solving. The campus's first academic plan provided for Divisions of Biological Sciences, Fine Arts, Humanities, Physical Sciences, and Social Sciences, as well as a School of Engineering and a Graduate School of Management.

UCI was dubbed the "instant university" for the speed with which it blossomed into a full-fledged institution of learning; its original enrollment of 1,589 has swelled to more than

Social Science Tower, UC Irvine. Photograph by Alan Nyiri.

23,000 undergraduate, graduate, and professional students. It now offers sixty-one undergraduate majors, as well as fifty-eight graduate and three professional programs. In 1995, UCI became the first public university to have two faculty members in different disciplines—chemistry and physics—awarded Nobel Prizes in the same year. In 1996, UC Irvine joined the ranks of the nation's top universities as a member of the Association of American Universities.

The UCI Medical Center, Orange County's only university hospital, includes a world-class cancer center as well as outstanding services in trauma and burn treatment, minimally invasive surgery, and neurological disease. The University Research Park is a realization of Aldrich's and Pereira's vision of UC Irvine as a magnet for scientists and entrepreneurs whose partnership with the campus would create new knowledge for UCI and new technologies and jobs for its community.

LOS ANGELES

UCLA, symbolized by the majestic towers of Royce Hall, ranks among the most distinguished universities in the United States.

In 1919 Governor William D. Stephens signed legislation transfering the buildings and grounds of the Los Angeles State Normal School on North Vermont Avenue to the University. Six years later, the present site in Westwood (now 419 acres) was chosen by the Regents as the Los Angeles campus, and classes began there in 1929.

Within four years the campus expanded its undergraduate offerings to include advanced study; professional training came soon thereafter. But it was after World War II that UCLA, along with the vibrant city of which it is so important a part, began its fastest period of growth. Today UCLA serves almost 37,000 students—among them more than 24,000 undergraduates. The College of Letters and Science, with eleven programs ranked among the top ten in their fields, is the largest and most comprehensive in the UC system. UCLA's eleven professional schools provide graduate training

Royce Hall, UCLA. Photograph by Alan Nyiri.

in the health sciences, law, education, engineering, management, public policy, and the arts. The UCLA Medical Center, which serves more than 300,000 patients every year, is consistently ranked as the best hospital in the western United States.

UCLA is a major research and economic engine for Southern California. The campus ranks third among colleges and universities in the United States in federal support for research and development; at any given time, more than 5,000 funded research projects are being conducted on campus. UCLA's academic excellence is reflected in its 1974 election to the Association of American Universities and the five Nobel Prize winners who have been members of its faculty.

Like Los Angeles itself, UCLA is one of the most diverse communities in the nation and a vital partner in the life of the surrounding city. It serves as a hub for culture, athletics, and lifelong learning. The campus offers acclaimed year-round programs of visual and performing arts. Its men's and women's varsity sports teams have won more national championships than those at any other American university. UCLA Extension, with 4,500 courses presented every year and an enrollment of more than 100,000, is the world's largest provider of nondegree higher education.

MERCED

Located in the San Joaquin Valley in the shadow of the magnificent Sierra Nevada, UC Merced is the University's youngest campus and the first major American research university of the twenty-first century. It is also the first UC campus in the San Joaquin Valley, with a special focus on serving the Valley's 3.5 million residents from Stockton to Bakersfield.

The campus is set on 2,000 scenic acres near Lake Yosemite; the remaining 5,000 acres will be kept as a natural reserve. Its founding Chancellor, Carol Tomlinson-Keasey, was appointed in 1999. UCM is expected to open in 2005 with an enrollment of 1,000 undergraduate and graduate students.

Planning and architecture for UC Merced will emphasize environmental friendliness and the use of digital technology to serve students and communities throughout the Central Valley. The campus will be organized around three academic divisions—engineering; natural sciences; and social sciences, humanities, and the arts. The first professional school will be the Ernest and Julio Gallo School of Management. The Leo and Dottie Kolligian Library, scheduled for opening in 2004, will be a state-of-the art facility housing both paper and digital collections.

UCM's first two research centers—the Sierra Nevada Re-

UC Merced. Photograph by Alan Nyiri.

search Institute and the World Cultures Institute—will use the diverse peoples of California and the ecosystems of the Central Valley and Sierra Nevada region as a laboratory for exploring issues of global import. Among those issues will be population growth and development, ecology, and the cultures and traditions that have made and remade California over its history.

UC Merced has already attracted support for fourteen endowed professorships and funding commitments from major foundations to help launch its academic programs.

RIVERSIDE

The Riverside campus began as the Citrus Experiment Station on twenty-three acres of land on Mount Rubidoux in 1907. Later renamed the Citrus Research Center and Agricultural Experiment Station, the school has been an invaluable source of research and training for California's young citrus industry. Work done at Riverside is credited with saving that industry for the state in the 1940s when the deadly tristeza virus hit.

In 1948 Governor Earl Warren, recognizing Southern California's burgeoning postwar demand for educational opportunity, signed legislation authorizing UC to open a campus at Riverside. A year later UCLA professor of economics Gordon S. Watkins was named Provost of the UCR campus, which was to focus on offering an undergraduate education equal to that of outstanding private liberal arts colleges. The first students—127 strong—were welcomed by the Provost and 65 faculty members in February of 1954.

UC Riverside was designated a general campus of the University in 1959, which meant that the campus could now

Carillon Tower, UC Riverside. Photograph by Alan Nyiri.

develop graduate and professional programs. The College of Agriculture opened in 1960, followed by the Dry Lands Research Institute and Air Pollution Research Center a year later. The campus's best-known landmark, the Carillon Tower, was dedicated in 1966, and its musical voice still rings over the campus. UCR professional schools include the A. Gary Anderson Graduate School of Management, the Bourns School of Engineering, and the Graduate School of Education.

Today UC Riverside is a thriving and intellectually vital campus with a student body of nearly 16,000, the most diverse in the UC system. Students can choose from among sixty-four bachelor's degree programs and graduate disciplines leading to forty-four master's and thirty-six Ph.D. degrees. To its reputation for superb undergraduate education, UCR has added growing scholarly and scientific distinction.

The Citrus Research Center and Agricultural Experiment Station is known throughout the world for its contributions to subtropical and arid agriculture. UCR's leadership in entomology, which includes experts in biological control, pesticide use, and genetic engineering of insects, is also tied to its agricultural roots. The campus is on the cutting edge of entomological research and is home to a unique new Insectory and Quarantine facility that permits the safe study of exotic organisms from around the world.

UCR ranks at the top among institutions with the most faculty members elected annually as fellows of the American Association for the Advancement of Science.

SAN DIEGO

The San Diego campus traces its origin to the closing years of the nineteenth century when zoologists at Berkeley set out to establish a marine station on the Pacific. In 1903, the Marine Biological Association was established at La Jolla. Nine years later it was made a part of the University as the Scripps Institution for Biological Research, which ultimately became the world-famous Scripps Institution of Oceanography.

In the late 1950s, the Regents approved a general campus at San Diego, with Scripps as the nucleus. Famed oceanographer Roger Revelle led the recruitment of founding faculty such as the Nobel Prize–winning chemist Harold Urey, future Nobelist Maria Mayer, and many members of the National Academy of Sciences.

At first, only graduate studies and degrees in the physical sciences were offered. In the fall of 1964 the campus opened for undergraduates. A special feature of the new campus, and one of its continuing strengths, is its residential college structure. Undergraduates complete their general education requirements in one of six residential colleges and benefit from the personal staffing, academic guidance, and community support that only a small college can provide.

Geisel Library, UC San Diego. Photograph by Alan Nyiri.

With an enrollment of more than 23,000 undergraduate, graduate, and professional students, UCSD is acknowledged to be the best institution of higher learning established in the U.S. since World War II. The campus was elected to membership in the Association of American Universities in 1982. Its faculty includes nine Nobel Laureates and one of the country's highest concentrations of members of the National Academies of Science, Engineering, and Medicine. UCSD is fifth nationally, and first in the UC system, in federal R&D expenditures, attracting annual research awards of more than $550 million.

The campus is a leader in many fields, including neurosciences, biological sciences, chemistry, theater, political science, and engineering. UCSD houses unique international resources such as the San Diego Supercomputer Center and the Center for U.S.-Mexican Studies.

UCSD's graduate schools include the Jacobs School of Engineering, the School of International Relations and Pacific Studies, and a Graduate Management School that opened in 2003. UCSD is home to a School of Medicine, a School of Pharmacy and Pharmaceutical Sciences, an innovative M.D.-Ph.D. program, and two hospitals.

The campus is situated on 1,200 spectacular acres of coastal woodland bordering the Pacific.

SAN FRANCISCO

The second-oldest campus of the University, San Francisco is the only one devoted exclusively to the health sciences. Hugh Toland, a leading practitioner in Gold Rush San Francisco, founded the Toland Medical College in 1864; it became the University's Medical Department in 1873, the same year the University also acquired the California College of Pharmacy. In 1881 a School of Dentistry was added—the first west of the Mississippi—followed by a School of Nursing in 1906. From a makeshift hospital set up in Golden Gate Park after the 1906 earthquake, the UCSF Medical Center has grown to become one of the finest in the nation.

UCSF's Mission Bay campus, situated on forty-three acres donated by the Catellus Development Corporation and the City and County of San Francisco, will open groundbreaking opportunities for collaborative, interdisciplinary research on the fundamental processes that underlie all forms of life. Mission Bay's advantages—UCSF's scientific excellence and leadership in biomedical research, the proximity of industry

Hippocrates, Crede Ambulatory Care Center, UCSF.
Photograph by Alan Nyiri.

partners, and its location in one of the great cities of the world—make it the nation's most exciting new center for investigation into the life sciences.

UCSF is distinguished by many pathbreaking achievements. In the 1970s, UCSF researchers collaborated with colleagues at Stanford University on the development of recombinant DNA techniques. Their astonishing breakthrough created the biotechnology industry and made the San Francisco Bay Area a world leader in biotechnology: some sixty biotechnology firms trace their origin to UC San Francisco.

Professor—later Chancellor—J. Michael Bishop and Professor Harold Varmus were awarded the 1989 Nobel Prize in Medicine for their discovery that normal cellular genes can be converted to cancer genes. Professor Stanley Prusiner won a 1997 Nobel Prize for his work on prions, an infectious agent responsible for a variety of neurodegenerative diseases. Other UCSF firsts include the development of prenatal tests for sickle-cell anemia, the development of a genetically engineered hepatitis B vaccine and synthetic human insulin to treat diabetes, and the first successful surgery on a baby still in the mother's womb.

UCSF includes 19 research institutes, 1,900 laboratories, more than 3,000 research projects, and a state-of-the-art library. Long ranked as a premier center for research, training, and patient care, UCSF is also a leader in attracting government and private research funds.

SANTA BARBARA

The Santa Barbara campus is located on 989 acres overlooking the Pacific Ocean ten miles up the coast from the city of Santa Barbara, with the dramatic Santa Ynez Mountains in the background.

Santa Barbara State College became a campus of the University in 1944 and was known as Santa Barbara College. A decade later, it was moved to the present site near Goleta, and in 1958 the College was authorized as a general campus of the University.

Today UCSB enrolls just under 20,000 undergraduate and graduate students. Its College of Letters and Science, the campus's largest, offers more than ninety majors. The College of Creative Studies gives talented undergraduates opportunities to do advanced, independent work in the arts and sciences. Engineering education in a variety of fields through the doctoral level is provided by the College of Engineering, and the Gevirtz Graduate School of Education includes a teacher credential program and advanced degrees in education. The Donald Bren School of Environmental Science and Management—the University's first multicampus professional school—is unique in its interdisciplinary approach to environmental problems and policy.

University Center, UC Santa Barbara. Photograph by Alan Nyiri.

The campus administers the university-wide Education Abroad Program, which since its founding in 1962 has given more than 40,000 UC students the opportunity to study at 140 institutions in thirty-four countries.

UC Santa Barbara's rise to national prominence is reflected in its 1995 election to the Association of American Universities, which comprises leading universities in the United States and Canada. In 1998, the Institute for Scientific Information placed the campus among the top ten national universities for the quality of scientific research by its faculty, based on the rate of citation by other scholars.

UCSB is the site of eight national centers and institutes, including the Kavli Institute for Theoretical Physics, the National Center for Ecological Analysis and Synthesis, and the Center for Middle East Studies. And it is home to three Nobel Laureates—two selected in the same year—and to many members of the National Academy of Sciences, the National Academy of Engineering, the National Endowment for the Humanities, and the American Academy of Arts and Sciences.

SANTA CRUZ

Located on a redwood-studded 2,000-acre site overlooking Monterey Bay, the Santa Cruz campus was planned by architect John Carl Warnecke and landscape architect Thomas Church to make the most of its superb natural setting. UCSC admitted its first class of 652 students in the fall of 1965. Today the campus enrolls more than 14,000 students who can choose from fifty-six majors in the humanities, natural sciences, engineering, social sciences, and arts. Graduate degrees are offered in twenty-seven academic fields and in engineering.

UCSC's residential colleges combine the advantages of living and learning in a small college setting with the scholarly resources of a large research university. Cowell College opened in 1965. Over the years, nine other residential colleges have been added, most recently College Ten, which opened in the fall of 2002. A distinctive aspect of undergraduate education at UC Santa Cruz is the practice of giving students written assessments of their performance in addition to letter grades.

Graduate study began in 1966 with programs in astronomy, biology, and history of consciousness and quickly expanded to include fields ranging from environmental studies

Redwood Building, Quarry Plaza, UC Santa Cruz.
Photograph by Alan Nyiri.

to philosophy. UCSC's first professional school, the Jack Baskin School of Engineering, opened in 1997.

The campus has established the UC Silicon Valley Center at NASA Ames to advance research partnerships, expand higher education–industry collaborations, and increase student access.

UC Santa Cruz is headquarters for the University of California Observatories/Lick Observatory, the national Center for Adaptive Optics, and the Laboratory for Adaptive Optics. It is home to a branch of the Institute of Geophysics and Planetary Physics, a multicampus research unit devoted to exploring the origin, structure, and evolution of the Earth, the solar system, and the universe. The Santa Cruz Institute for Particle Physics focuses on theoretical and experimental projects concerning fundamental interactions of matter.

The Institute of Marine Sciences sponsors the Center for Ocean Health, performing research in coastal marine biology, paleoceanography, and many other areas. The New Teacher Center has developed a nationally recognized model for teacher training. The Center for Global, International, and Regional Studies takes an interdisciplinary approach to complex economic, social, and political issues.

The excellence of the campus's teaching and research has been recognized by many measures. UCSC students and alumni have won National Science Foundation fellowships, Fulbrights, Mellon Foundation Fellowships in the Humanities, and other prestigious awards in numbers far out of proportion to the size of the campus.

PRESIDENTS OF
THE UNIVERSITY OF CALIFORNIA

John LeConte	Acting President, 1869–70
Henry Durant	1870–72
Daniel Coit Gilman	1872–75
John LeConte	Acting President, 1875–76
	President, 1876–81
William Thomas Reid	1881–85
Edward Singleton Holden	1885–88
Horace Davis	1888–90
Martin Kellogg	Acting President, 1890–93
	President, 1893–99
Benjamin Ide Wheeler	1899–1919
David Prescott Barrows	1919–23
William Wallace Campbell	1923–30
Robert Gordon Sproul	1930–58
Clark Kerr	1958–67
Harry R. Wellman	Acting President, 1967
Charles J. Hitch	1968–75
David S. Saxon	1975–83
David Pierpont Gardner	1983–92
Jack W. Peltason	1992–95
Richard C. Atkinson	1995–2003
Robert C. Dynes	2003–

CHIEF CAMPUS OFFICERS/CHANCELLORS OF THE UNIVERSITY OF CALIFORNIA

BERKELEY

Founded: 1868

Chancellor Clark Kerr, 1952–58
Chancellor Glenn T. Seaborg, 1958–61
Chancellor Edward W. Strong, 1961–65
Acting Chancellor Martin Meyerson, 1965
Chancellor Roger W. Heyns, 1965–71
Chancellor Albert H. Bowker, 1971–80
Chancellor Ira Michael Heyman, 1980–90
Chancellor Chang-Lin Tien, 1990–97
Chancellor Robert M. Berdahl, 1997–2004

DAVIS

Founded: 1905 as the University Farm to provide training in agriculture; became a general campus in 1959; until 1952 was administered by the Dean of Agriculture at Berkeley

Chancellor Stanley B. Freeborn,
Provost 1952–58, Chancellor 1958–59
Chancellor Emil M. Mrak, 1959–69

Chancellor James H. Meyer, 1969–87
Chancellor Theodore L. Hullar, 1987–94
Chancellor Larry N. Vanderhoef, 1994–

IRVINE

Founded: 1965

Chancellor Daniel G. Aldrich Jr., 1962–84
Chancellor Jack W. Peltason, 1984–92
Acting Chancellor L. Dennis Smith, 1992–93
Chancellor Laurel L. Wilkening, 1993–98
Chancellor Ralph J. Cicerone, 1998–

LOS ANGELES

*Founded: 1919, when the Los Angeles State Normal School,
founded in 1881, became part of the University of California*

Vice President and Provost Ernest Carroll Moore,
Director 1919–30, Vice President and Director 1930–31,
Vice President and Provost, 1931–36
Vice President and Provost Earle R. Hedrick, 1937–42
Provost Clarence A. Dykstra, 1945–50
Chancellor Raymond B. Allen, 1952–59
Chancellor Vern O. Knudsen, 1959–60
Chancellor Franklin D. Murphy, 1960–68
Chancellor Charles E. Young, 1968–97
Chancellor Albert Carnesale, 1997–

MERCED

Founded: 1995

Chancellor Carol Tomlinson-Keasey, 1999–

RIVERSIDE

Founded: 1907 as Citrus Experiment Station;
became a campus in 1954

Provost Gordon Watkins, 1949–56
Chancellor Herman Spieth,
Provost 1956–58, Chancellor 1958–64
Chancellor Ivan Hinderaker, 1964–79
Chancellor Tomás Rivera, 1979–84
Acting Chancellor Daniel G. Aldrich Jr., 1984–85
Chancellor Theodore L. Hullar, 1985–87
Chancellor Rosemary S. J. Schraer, 1987–92
Chancellor Raymond L. Orbach, 1992–2002
Chancellor France A. Córdova, 2002–

SAN DIEGO

Founded: 1912 as marine station (later known as Scripps
Institution of Oceanography); became a general campus in 1959

Chancellor Herbert F. York, 1961–65
Chancellor John S. Galbraith, 1965–68
Chancellor William J. McGill, 1968–70
Acting Chancellor Herbert F. York, 1970–71
Chancellor William D. McElroy, 1971–80
Chancellor Richard C. Atkinson, 1980–95
Acting Chancellor Marjorie Caserio, 1995–96
Chancellor Robert C. Dynes, 1996–2003
Acting Chancellor Marsha Chandler, 2003–

Founded: 1864 as a private medical college; in 1873, became part of the University of California; prior to 1954, deans of various schools reported to the President of the University; beginning in 1954 an administrative advisory committee was formed, headed by the dean of medicine (1954–58)

Chancellor John B. de C. M. Saunders,
Provost 1958–64, Chancellor 1964–66
Chancellor Willard C. Fleming, 1966–69
Chancellor Philip R. Lee, 1969–72
Chancellor Francis A. Sooy, 1972–82
Chancellor Julius R. Krevans, 1983–93
Chancellor Joseph B. Martin, 1993–97
Chancellor Haile Debas, 1997–98
Chancellor J. Michael Bishop, 1998–

SANTA BARBARA

Founded: 1909 as a State Normal School (predecessor institution founded in 1901 as the Anna S. C. Blake Manual Training School); in 1920, was renamed the Santa Barbara State Teachers College; in 1944, became Santa Barbara College of the University of California; became a general campus in 1958

Provost Clarence L. Phelps, 1944–46
Provost J. Harold Williams, 1946–55
Provost Clark G. Kuebler, 1955
Acting Provost John C. Snidecor, 1956
Acting Provost Elmer R. Noble, 1956–59
Chancellor Samuel B. Gould, 1959–62
Chancellor Vernon I. Cheadle, 1962–77

Acting Chancellor Alec Alexander, 1977
Chancellor Robert A. Huttenback, 1977–86
Acting Chancellor Daniel G. Aldrich Jr., 1986–87
Chancellor Barbara S. Uehling, 1987–94
Chancellor Henry T. Yang, 1994–

SANTA CRUZ

Founded: 1965

Chancellor Dean E. McHenry, 1961–74
Chancellor Mark N. Christensen, 1974–76
Acting Chancellor Angus E. Taylor, 1976–77
Chancellor Robert L. Sinsheimer, 1977–87
Chancellor Robert Stevens, 1987–91
Chancellor Karl S. Pister, 1991–96
Chancellor M. R. C. Greenwood, 1996–2004
Acting Chancellor Martin M. Chemers, 2004–

NOTES

1. William Carey Jones, *Illustrated History of the University of California* (San Francisco, 1895), p. 56.

2. Jones, p. 59.

3. Quoted in Francesco Cordasco, *Daniel Coit Gilman and the Protean Ph.D.: The Shaping of American Graduate Education* (Leiden: E. J. Brill, 1960), p. 35.

4. Edwin E. Slosson, *Great American Universities* (New York, 1910), p. 149.

5. Slosson, p. 180.

6. John Aubrey Douglass, *The California Idea and American Higher Education, 1850 to the 1960 Master Plan* (Stanford, 2000), p. 105.

7. Douglass, p. 133.

8. Angus E. Taylor, *The Academic Senate of the University of California: Its Role in the Shared Governance and Operation of the University of California* (Berkeley, 1998), p. 4.

9. Robert Gordon Sproul, remarks during annual alumni tour, 1950

10. Verne Stadtman, ed., *The Centennial Record of the University of California* (Berkeley, 1967), p. 406.

11. Eugene C. Lee, *The Origins of the Chancellorship* (Berkeley, 1995), p. 28.

12. Clark Kerr, "The Idea of a Multiversity," *The Uses of the University* (Cambridge, Mass., 1963), p. 1.

13. Kerr, p. 45.

14. Kerr, p. 42.

15. Sheldon Rothblatt, ed., *The OECD, the Master Plan, and the California Dream* (Berkeley, 1992), p. 45.

16. Clark Kerr, *The Gold and the Blue: A Personal Memoir of the University of California, 1949–1967,* vol. 1, *Academic Triumphs* (Berkeley, 2001), p. 203.

17. Professor Leon Litwack, remarks at the dedication of the Sproul Hall steps, December 3, 1997.

18. Charles J. Hitch, "Missions Impossible," Charter Day remarks at UCLA, April 3, 1975.

19. Peter Schrag, *Paradise Lost: California's Experience, America's Future* (New York, 1998), p. 154.

20. David Saxon, "Report on Universitywide Planning Initiatives," Regents' meeting, January 19, 1979.

21. Schrag, p. 160.

22. "The University of California: A Multi-Campus System in the 1980s," report of the Joint Planning Committee, Office of the President, September 1979, p. C1-1.

23. David P. Gardner, remarks to the Board of Regents, October 20, 1988.

24. David P. Gardner, "Summary Statement to the Regents pertaining to the Report by the State Auditor General," Regents' meeting, November 20, 1987.

25. Marvin L. Goldberger et al., eds., *Research Doctorate Programs in the United States: Continuity and Change,* National Research Council, 1995.

26. Hugh Davis Graham and Nancy Diamond, *The Rise of American Research Universities: Elites and Challengers in the Postwar Era* (Baltimore and London, 1997), p. 149.

27. *New Directions for Outreach: Report of the UC Outreach Task Force,* p. 14.

28. Richard C. Atkinson, "The California Crucible: Demography, Excellence, and Access at the University of California," Keynote

Address, International Assembly of the Council for Advancement and Support of Education, San Francisco, July 2, 2001.

29. Richard C. Atkinson, "Standardized Tests and Access to American Universities," 2001 Robert H. Atwell Distinguished Lecture, 83rd Annual Meeting, American Council on Education, Washington, D.C., February 18, 2001.

FURTHER READING

Adams, Ansel, and Newhall, Nancy. *Fiat Lux: The University of California, A Centennial Publication.* New York: McGraw-Hill, 1967.

Anderson, Nancy Scott. *An Improbable Venture: A History of the University of California, San Diego.* La Jolla: UCSD Press, 1993.

Dickinson, Edward Augustus. *University of California at Los Angeles: Its Origin and Formative Years.* Los Angeles: Friends of the UCLA Library, 1955.

Douglass, John A. *The California Idea and American Higher Education, 1850 to the 1960 Master Plan.* Stanford, Calif.: Stanford University Press, 2000.

Ferrier, William Warren. *Origin and Development of the University of California.* Berkeley: Sather Gate Book Shop, 1937.

Gardner, David Pierpont. *The California Oath Controversy.* Berkeley: University of California Press, 1967.

Johnson, Dean C. *The University of California: History and Achievements.* Berkeley: UC Printing Services, University of California, 1996.

Kelley, Robert. *Transformations: UC Santa Barbara 1909–1979.* Santa Barbara, Calif.: Associated Students, University of California, 1981.

Kerr, Clark. *The Gold and the Blue: A Personal Memoir of the University of California, 1949–1967.* Vol. 1: *Academic Triumphs.* Berkeley: University of California Press, 2001.

———. *The Gold and the Blue: A Personal Memoir of the University of California, 1949–1967.* Vol. 2: *Political Turmoil.* Berkeley: University of California Press, 2003.

———. *The Uses of the University.* 5th ed. Cambridge: Harvard University Press, 2001.

McCulloch, Samuel Clyde. *Instant University: The History of the University of California, Irvine, 1957–1993.* Irvine: University of California, 1994.

McGill, William J. *The Year of the Monkey: Revolt on Campus, 1968–69.* New York: McGraw-Hill, 1982.

Pettitt, George A. *Twenty-eight Years in the Life of a University President.* Berkeley: University of California Press, 1966.

Pickerell, Albert, and Dornin, May. *The University of California: A Pictorial History.* A Centennial Publication of the University of California, 1968.

Rothblatt, Sheldon, ed. *The OECD, the Master Plan, and the California Dream: A Berkeley Conversation.* Berkeley: Center for Studies in Higher Education, 1992.

Scheuring, Ann F. *Abundant Harvest: The History of the University of California, Davis.* Davis: UC Davis History Project, 2001.

Schrag, Peter. *Paradise Lost: California's Experience and America's Future.* New York: New Press, 1998.

Stadtman, Verne A., ed. *The Centennial Record of the University of California: 1868–1968.* Berkeley: University of California Press, 1967.

———. *The University of California, 1868–1968.* New York: McGraw-Hill, 1970.

Taylor, Angus. *The Academic Senate of the University of California: Its Role in the Shared Governance and Operation of the University of California.* Berkeley: Institute of Governmental Studies, 1998.

Designer/Compositor:	Barbara Jellow Design
Text:	10/13 Adobe Garamond
Display:	Centaur Italic
Text printer and Binder:	Edwards Brothers, Inc.
Jacket Printer:	Pinnacle Press, Inc.